THE LIVERPOOL STORY

THE LIVERPOOL STORY

Derek Hodgson

Arthur Barker Limited   London
A Subsidiary of Weidenfeld (Publishers) Limited

Contents

Foreword

By John W. Smith, JP
Chairman, Liverpool Association Football Club

I am delighted to welcome the publication of this book because a history of this nature has been needed for many years. I am sure I speak on behalf of all members of the Board and the staff in greeting *The Liverpool Story*.

I am only sorry that our late and first president Mr Tom Williams is not alive to see this publication. He was always very keen on recording our history and I feel sure he would have been impressed and gratified by Derek Hodgson's work.

Memories brought back by the book will interest all our readers and supporters and evoke many happy times for those able to remember the pre-war days and the 1920s.

Liverpool have always been a personal club, a family club, and one reason for our success is that we have always believed that people matter most, a sentiment that *The Liverpool Story* has faithfully captured.

It gives me great pleasure in commending this book to all our supporters throughout the world and, indeed, to all lovers of the game of football.

Anfield
February 1978

Acknowledgments

The illustrations in this book are reproduced by kind permission of the following:

London Express: 23, 55t, 61b, 62, 63, 64, 65, 67, 72, 73, 74, 76, 77, 79, 80, 82, 86, 87, 89t, 91, 93b, 95t, 96, 102, 105, 109, 111, 112, 117b, 120, 123b, 127t, 149t, 149b.

Liverpool Daily Post & Echo: 11, 16, 17, 25t, 26, 32, 35, 39b, 40, 45, 46, 48, 51, 53, 55b, 58, 69, 70, 81, 84, 89b, 93t, 95b, 98, 103, 106, 116, 117t, 123t, 127b, 131, 134, 137, 141, 143.

Radio Times Hulton Picture Library: 22, 25b, 29, 30, 33, 36, 37, 39t, 41, 43, 49, 56, 61t.

1

King John, Honest John

Had Karl Marx lived in Kirkby in the spring of 1977 he might have re-written his famous aphorism to read: 'Football is the opium of the people.' Western Europe was gripped by recession, unemployment figures soared. The red, white and blue bunting to celebrate Elizabeth II's Silver Jubilee flew over mean streets of gnawing poverty on Merseyside. Yet for a fort-night this grey, rain-washed river city was a world of woozy song, awash with sentiment, bleary-eyed with celebration. From the raggedy urchins who swarm, squirrel-like, on the Kop to the mink-and-diamond-clad wives in the directors' boxes, the word had been 'Liverpool'.

In May 1977, the Liverpool Association Football Club emerged as the most successful in the eighty-nine-year history of the Football League. By 15 May the League championship had been retained, making ten championships in all, a record. On 22 May Liverpool lost the FA Cup Final to Manchester United, but a journey to Wembley is never a failure, always, win or lose, a day to sing about. Four days later, in the capital of the Caesars, Liverpool became champions of Europe. Even the fastidious Romans, who had feared the coming of Kevin Keegan and the Kop as their forebears had feared Alaric and his Goths, joined the festivities.

It was an astonishing, glorious fourteen days in the history of a club born without a name and weaned in a crisis of identity. For if John Hould-ing, the founder of the club, had had his way there would have been no Liverpool football club. The present empire was built from the frustra-tions of a formidable man. Houlding was a brewer who became a city

9

alderman, a Justice of the Peace and Lord Mayor. He was also a landlord in the Anfield Road area, owning the area of the ground and the nearby Sandon Hotel.

Houlding was known in the city as 'King John of Everton'. An enthusiastic supporter of the club founded at St Domingo's Sunday School in 1878, Houlding became their landlord when Everton moved to Anfield in 1884 and was a prime mover in their becoming one of the original twelve members of the Football League four years later. But by 1892 a growing rift between Houlding and his fellow Evertonians had become a breach. When a dispute arose over the rent for the Anfield ground the majority seized the opportunity to buy some land on what is now Goodison Park and moved out. Houlding refused to give up. He firstly insisted on retaining the name of 'Everton' and the Football League had to rule, on 26 February 1892, that the club's name stayed with the majority of members. He carried his fight to the FA who gave a similar ruling. So what to call the new club at Anfield? There was, after all, a Liverpool Football Club, playing Rugby Union but Houlding and his men decided that, despite protests, there would be a second Liverpool FC, the title 'Association' being added to prevent confusion. So on 15 March 1892, the new club was launched. Their colours were royal blue and white quarters (Everton were then in 'ruby' shirts). A Mr W. E. Barclay is recorded as the first secretary and guess who was president?

The fledgeling club had every reason to be grateful to the old autocrat who put £500 into the treasury and never pressed for repayment. 'He was a generous, life-long friend,' said the *Book of Football* (1906), 'and they had not too many of that sort. The "gates" were poor.' So poor in fact that when Liverpool played Rotherham, in their very first match (they lost 6–0) they could not meet the Yorkshire club's financial guarantee. Then, at the end of a first, triumphant season when they won both the Lancashire League and the Liverpool Cup, scoring sixty-six goals to nineteen, both the trophies awarded for winning these competitions were stolen. The cost of replacement, a heart-breaking setback to a struggling club, was £127.

At this point in the story John Houlding marches, steadfastly and implacably no doubt, into history and the Houlding Street that bears his name. While John McKenna appears. McKenna, like Houlding, was another of those sterling Victorians who believed in Samuel Smiles. An Ulster immigrant, he had begun his life in Liverpool as a nineteen-year-

John McKenna, the empire builder who established a tradition of buying Scottish players.

BELOW LEFT Matt McQueen, 1898, an original Scot.

BELOW RIGHT Tom Watson, a founder figure.

old grocery delivery boy and became, by various business enterprises, a rich man. McKenna became a committee member of the new club and then set off on what is surely the greatest recruiting trip in football history. In all he signed thirteen Scottish professionals, including Wyllie from Rangers; Hannah, McBride, McLean, Kelso and Cameron from Renton; Miller from Dumbarton and McVean from Third Lanark. That first team, in fact, became MacLiverpool. Registered players were Matt McQueen, Hugh McQueen, William McOwen, Duncan McLean, John McCartney, Joe McQue, John McBride and Malcolm McVean. Every time a Liverpool manager crosses the border to sign another Scot the ghost of John McKenna must travel with him.

McKenna realised immediately that his new club must win a Football League place as soon as possible. An application to join the new Second Division in the autumn of 1892 was rejected, hence the season in the Lancashire League. So a second application was made for the 1893–4 season at a time when the Second Division was to be extended to fifteen clubs. Liverpool still had a struggle for recognition. Although Accrington resigned before the season started Liverpool were only admitted through the demise of their neighbours – and much more famous rivals – Bootle.

Bootle had won attention by their enterprising recruiting, taking Welshmen from the famous Druids of Ruabon, players from Essex and from all parts of Lancashire at a time when no transfer system existed. Local rivalry must have been intense for in 1882 Everton claimed a Liverpool Cup tie after unruly Bootle supporters invaded the pitch during play. Perhaps Bootle over-reached themselves in their one season in the League (1892). The Directors, it was recorded, had already spent £120 but had scanty support for their efforts.

News of the green pastures on Merseyside had obviously swept through Scotland for, as the Bootle club went down, an ex-Celtic forward offered his services for '£8 down, £3 a week and 25s during the close season'. With Bootle gone, McKenna won a place in the League for his Liverpool. The other four newcomers were Arsenal, Middlesbrough Ironopolis (not today's Middlesbrough), Newcastle United and Rotherham United. Liverpool had established their name. The renown that followed was swift and startling.

From 1 September 1893 to 30 April 1894 the new Liverpool lost only five matches in all competitions, a record that bears comparison with the days of Shankly and Paisley. The Second Division was a romp, for Liverpool won all but two of their twenty-eight League games, starting with a 2–0 win at Ironopolis and drawing 'a capital crowd' of 5,000 for their first home game, a 4–0 win over Lincoln. They also had a thrilling and for those days astonishing FA Cup victory, by 3–2, over Preston at Anfield and in those days North End were rightly known as the 'Invincibles'. All Liverpool's home games were won, forty-six goals being scored to six against and the club finished eight points clear at the top of the Second Division.

Promotion was not then automatic but in the Test Matches against the club at the bottom of the First, Newton Heath (soon to reappear under a much more dangerous name) Liverpool were successful and entered the First Division in only their second season in the League. The sheer drudgery of working-class life in Victorian times is reflected in the figures for convictions for drunkenness – 15,000 a year in the city – and one would be happy to think that some proportion were celebrating Liverpool's success. There was every excuse to drown sorrows the following season. Liverpool's first experience of the First Division was a bitter one, winning only six home games, only two away, finishing bottom, losing the Test Match to Bury and thus being immediately relegated. The first derby, at Goodison, drew 44,000, Everton winning 3–0 and there were another 27,000 to see the rivals draw 2–2 at Anfield in the return, extraordinarily high attendances at a time when poverty was all too real and the only social security was the workhouse. Liverpool were not so much outclassed in the First Division as short on luck. Injuries were so prevalent the club could not field the same team in successive matches. 'It is combination rather than individual excellence that wins League matches. One "star" among ten "sticks" is no use except for stage purposes,' observed the *Book of Football* magisterially.

The club must have had its perilous moments off the field. In the darkest days of the relegation season 'there were not enough spectators to go round the field' recorded one sad observer. The fine grandstand, erected to hold 3,000 at a cost of £1,000, was often almost empty. There were even rumours of attempts to steal away Liverpool's better players but the new president, Mr W. Houlding, son of the old man, persuaded McKenna and his committee not to part with a single player.

Relegation was hard to swallow for John McKenna. Stung, he repeated the successful formula of two years before: 'Send for the Scots.' George

Allan, a mercurial talent – he died at twenty four – came from Leith and became Liverpool's first Scottish international when he was capped two years later. Archie Goldie arrived from Clyde, Frank Becton, already an England player, and Jimmy Ross, 'fast, brilliant and a deadly shot', wrote a contemporary, were the first stars to make the short journey from Deepdale to Anfield.

Once again, Liverpool were much too good for a Second Division now increased to sixteen clubs and including some much more familiar names – both the Manchester clubs, Newcastle and Arsenal, along with such forgotten heroes as Darwen, Burton Wanderers and Burton Swifts. McKenna's rebuilding brought sensational results. Only one home point – a goal-less draw with Darwen – was dropped, twenty-two matches were won and only one other game, away, drawn. The goal-scoring won Liverpool fame. Rotherham were beaten 10–1 (Allan scored four), Burton Swifts and Crewe were each beaten 7–0 away and there were a string of runaway home games. Liverpool hit 106 League goals that season, still a club record and although the new Manchester City matched them for points (forty-six) Liverpool's goal average was immeasurably superior. Liverpool also sailed through the Test Matches, taking five points from four games against Small Heath and West Bromwich and were once more back in the First Division after three hectic seasons.

The 1896–7 season, with Liverpool now in red shirts and white shorts, facing tougher opposition, was one of respectable consolidation. The gap in class between the two divisions was apparent in that the Liverpool century-scorers were confined to forty-six against the better-organised defences of the First Division. Liverpool finished fifth but the real excitement that season came from the club's first FA Cup run. Burton Swifts, West Bromwich and Forest were beaten on their way to the semi-final. As Everton also reached the semi-final Merseyside was agog with the thought of a Cup Final meeting at Crystal Palace. Everton obliged by beating Derby 3–2 at Stoke, but Liverpool were outclassed by Aston Villa before a 30,000 crowd at the Sheffield United ground and Villa went on to complete the first Champions–Cupwinners' double by defeating Everton in the Final.

By now Liverpool's status was being recognised in other directions. Allan was capped for Scotland (against England), Becton for England (against Wales) and the left winger Harry Bradshaw played for England and the Football League. Allan was then tempted back to Scotland, to

Celtic, returned to Anfield in 1898, but then caught a fatal chest complaint.

'Honest' John McKenna was satisfied, temporarily. The club had survived a stormy second season and was now established and recognised. The big prizes might still be a distance away but they were in sight.

The League Championship Cup with T. V. Williams and RIGHT in 1922, with Andy McGuigan (seated) and trainer Charlie Wilson.

LIVERPOOL
FOOTBALL CLUB.
LEAGUE CHAMPIONS

2

Safe and Steady Sam

Liverpool were a highly respectable ninth in the First Division of 1897–8 and also reached the last eight of the FA Cup. For the first time Everton were beaten (3–1) at Anfield but the Blues had their revenge with a 3–0 victory at Goodison. The Cup run ended in disaster. Liverpool had forced a 1–1 draw at the Baseball Ground before Steve Bloomer and the Derby attack wrecked Anfield in the replay, winning 5–1.

The following season was rich in incident, Liverpool falling, twice, just short of a summit. It was remembered as the year of Sheffield United. In the League match at Anfield Sheffield United's twenty-stone goalkeeper Willie Foulke, known as 'Man Mountain', suddenly seized George Allan, who had charged him, by his legs and stood him on his head in the mud, bouncing him up and down.

This was the extraordinary prelude to a classic Cup contest between the clubs in the semi-final. The serial began with a 2–2 draw at Nottingham Forest and another 4–4, at Bolton, where Liverpool led 2–0 and 4–2. The FA then turned to Fallowfield, Manchester, for the second replay thinking, perhaps, that a Monday afternoon in Manchester would not be too attractive. In the event an estimated 30,000 tried to get into a ground much too small for such a crowd, who kept spilling over on to the pitch. By half-time, with Liverpool leading by a goal from Allan, the referee abandoned the game, the 45 minutes having grown, with interruptions, to 105. The next stop, the following Thursday, was at Derby where Sheffield won by the only goal with only five minutes left.

The disappointment was intense, but Liverpool kept their momentum

in the League and forced the decision on the destination of the championship to the very last match. Liverpool had to travel to Villa. Both clubs
had forty-three points, with Villa having the fractionally better goal
average. Well-matched as they may have been Liverpool were then playing their sixteenth match in forty-three days – and those were days of
long travel. Villa won 5–0, all their goals coming in the first thirty-five
minutes and the receipts, from the League's record gate of 41,357, were
£1,500!

Another link, at that time, with Sheffield United, was the signing of
'Rab' Howell, believed to be the only true Romany ever to play for England. Howell was born in a caravan near Sheffield and after leaving United
for Liverpool, returned to caravan life when his football career was over.
Alex Raisbeck was another important recruit that season, a player destined
to become one of the great Scotland centre-halves. Raisbeck, like a famous
successor, came from a large family of miners and was originally signed
by Stoke, but then returned home. He was persuaded to return and sign
for Liverpool by the man who had replaced John McKenna as talent-
spotter, secretary-manager Tom Watson.

Watson began in football as secretary to Newcastle West End, a prede-
cessor of the famous United. From 1887 to 1896 he was secretary of Sunderland and was regarded as the inspiration behind their three League
championships and the mighty 'team of all the talents'. His translation
to Liverpool in August 1896 was clearly a major capture, planned, no
doubt, by the shrewd McKenna. Their team-building did not bring immediate results, Liverpool finishing tenth and suffering a second-round
Cup knockout in 1899–1900, but the sun broke through brilliantly in the
first season of the new century.

The League start was no more than average, but their finish was sensational, dropping only three points in their last twelve games. Sunderland's
lead was still sufficient to cause another last-match finish to the championship when Liverpool, needing only one point to defeat the relegated West
Bromwich, won 1–0. I think it is safe to say that never again will a club
win the Football League championship only eight years after its admission
to the League. Only eighteen players were used, the redoubtable Raisbeck
missing only three matches, and Liverpool seemed set for a long period
of glory and prosperity, attracting as they were the large average attendance of 18,000.

The setback came in the first of the periodical financial arguments that rock football. On 1 April 1901, the Football League ruled that the maximum wage for a player should be £4 a week, together with a fixed signing-on fee of £10. It was a laudable attempt by the League to regulate the undoubted poaching of players that had been rife since before the League was founded, giving all clubs an equal chance to compete through payment of a transfer fee. But to a club such as Liverpool, who under McKenna's far-seeing administration, had always paid liberal bonuses – the championship team were estimated to have averaged £10 a week, an enormous sum then – the new rules were a blow. Some footballers left the game completely and others, particularly the public school and university element who might have been attracted by unrestricted earnings, followed their own professions and by-passed League football.

Nevertheless following Liverpool through the golden age of the Edwardians, was eventful. They rarely had what might be called a dull season. They scored only forty-two goals in the First Division of 1901–2, but seven came all in one game in January when Stoke, hit by food poisoning, were reduced to seven men. Andy McGuigan scored five times for Liverpool, a feat not equalled until 1954, when John Evans scored five against Bristol Rovers. In December 1903 Grimsby were beaten 9–2, but Liverpool failed to heed the warnings of two seasons of low scoring overall. Once the defence cracked – sixty-two goals were conceded in 1903–4 – the team were struggling and relegation followed.

Recruitment followed: Jack Parkinson, born in Bootle and joining the club as an amateur, entered the first team to score twenty-four goals. Sam Raybould, formerly of Chesterfield and New Brighton, arrived to score nineteen and R. Robinson (Sunderland) hit twenty-four in a total of ninety-three. In only one game, a 2–0 defeat at Bolton, did Liverpool fail to score. The last five matches were won with a goal aggregate of 17–1 and the total of twenty-seven victories was not equalled until 1961–2, in all a triumphal return to the First Division. The defence, too, had been strengthened by the signing of Sunderland's great Scottish goalkeeper, Teddy Doig, after fourteen seasons at Roker.

Everton, meanwhile, had been building a Cup reputation. They knocked out Liverpool in 1905, the winning shot coming from Harold Hardman, who later won greater fame as chairman of Manchester United. Everton reached the semi-final that year, but it was in 1905–6 that Merseyside rang with glory. While newly promoted Liverpool stormed on to win their second League championship, Everton defeated a fine Newcastle

United team in the Cup Final. For the first time football's two major trophies were in one city and Merseyside had to wait until 1966 for it to happen again.

The years 1905–12 were also the time of Sam Hardy. Sam, first of the great line of Chesterfield goalkeepers, joined Liverpool on their return to the First Division as Teddy Doig's pupil. Standing over six feet, Hardy learned so well and so quickly from the shrewd Scot that he displaced him in the first team and went on to become England's premier goalkeeper, gaining thirteen caps while at Anfield and another eleven at Aston Villa, a total equivalent to around one hundred internationals today. He had a quiet personality, on and off the field and his dislike of the spectacular caused him to be known as 'Safe and Steady Sam'. But he was an artist in his judgement and in the opinion of several old England players, up to his death in 1966, Sam Hardy was ranked first.

Another great Anfield character appeared that season, Joe Hewitt from Sunderland, who scored twenty-two from outside left or centre-forward. Joe spent more than sixty years with Liverpool, as player, coach and handyman and was joined in the team by a crowd favourite, Enoch West, from Burnley, soon to be known as 'Knocker'.

Even more eventful, perhaps more so in the history of the club than winning a second championship, was the building and opening, albeit without a roof, of a new steeply rising stand, known, because of the Boer War, as Spion Kop. The modern Liverpool was taking shape for, to celebrate the championship, comes the first mention of the club in Europe, the directors taking the team to Paris as a celebration.

The euphoria was short-lived. Liverpool were unable to maintain their supremacy, only occasionally displaying their full talents as when, in 1907–8, they shattered prospective champions Manchester United 7–4. by 1908–9 Liverpool had slipped into danger again. Raisbeck and the Welsh international trio of Maurice Parry, E. Peake and George Lathom were all reaching retirement and changes had to be made as relegation was avoided by only two points. Fortunately Jack Parkinson re-emerged as a regular scorer, joining Hardy in the England team in a season in which he scored thirty goals.

There were some remarkable matches in 1909–10. Newcastle led 5–2 at half-time at Anfield – and lost 6–5! Liverpool opened the new Old Trafford ground of Manchester United by winning 4–3 and also beat Forest 7–3. On Christmas Day 1909, Liverpool discovered that Hardy

ABOVE Eph Longworth, full-back and captain of both Liverpool and England, July 1926.

RIGHT Goalkeeper Kenny Campbell, eight Scotland caps, four hundred League matches.

and two deputy goalkeepers were injured. Left-half Jim Bradley was conscripted – and Bolton were beaten 3–0. Then, up from Leyton came Eph Longworth. Eph, who came from Bolton, had joined the London club but wanted to return and happily accepted Liverpool's offer. He stayed with the club eighteen years and formed, with Scottish international Don McKinlay, who arrived that Christmas 1909, a full-back partnership that lasted eighteen years. Eph also had the distinction, up until 1976, of being the only Liverpool player to captain England, an honour since given Kevin Keegan and Emlyn Hughes. Two more excellent defenders, Bob Pursell and Harry Lowe, arrived from Queen's Park and Gainsborough Trinity respectively, Lowe becoming club captain.

After a mediocre 1910–11 the team had another shake-up in 1912. Sam Hardy and centre-half Jimmy Harrower were transferred to Aston Villa and Tom Watson was despatched to Scotland again. This time he returned with the Cambuslang goalkeeper Kenny Campbell who, although overtaken by Elisha Scott, still won eight Scotland caps and played in almost four hundred matches for Liverpool, Leicester, Stoke and New Brighton.

Liverpool also managed to put one across Everton that season, although they couldn't anticipate how well they would emerge from a transfer exchange. Everton wanted Liverpool's outside-left Harold Uren and on 12 February 1912 proposed paying a fee plus two players, winger Tommy Gracey and Bill Lacey, a stocky little Irish utility player from Shelbourne. The deal was done, Uren faded out of the game while Lacey flourished, winning twenty-four caps for Ireland and playing in four different positions for Liverpool over sixteen years.

Anfielders were having a disturbing and worrying time. The team was still being chopped and changed around and, looking at the League form, to no good purpose. Parkinson, the England centre-forward, was vulnerable to injury and often out of the team for long spells. Relegation threatened in 1912 and was avoided only by taking a point from Oldham in the last match.

There were more cheerful signs in 1913 as Liverpool crept up to twelfth, although the gap between them and the champions Sunderland was emphasised by the scores in the two League meetings – 7–0 and 5–2! Villa beat Sunderland in the Cup Final that year, winning 1–0 before a 120,000 crowd at Crystal Palace. In those days the FA did not issue Cup Final tickets, deciding quite rightly that the huge Palace arena could accommodate all those who wished to see the match. Liverpool's interest in these

Everton's giveaway, Bill Lacey.
He played for Liverpool for
sixteen years.

England *v* Wales at Cardiff, 1921:
Tommy Bromilow is on the right
of the back row. Harry Chambers
is second from the left in the front
row.

Don McKinlay, pillar of Scotland.

details was quickened as the 1913–14 season developed into a Cup run. It started ingloriously enough, Liverpool being held 1–1 at home by Barnsley while Everton were being knocked out by Glossop. Then Liverpool began to move with purpose. Barnsley were beaten at Oakwell, Gillingham 2–0, West Ham 1–1 and 5–1 and then Queen's Park Rangers 2–1 at Anfield. The semi-final against Villa at White Hart Lane was thought to be such a formality that only 27,000 spectators, turned up, although observers at the time pointed out that it was foolish to play a semi-final in London on the same day as such a counter attraction as the Boat Race. Football was shaken when the result filtered through, Villa, with the great Hardy in goal, being beaten 2–0, Liverpool's goals coming from outside-left Jimmy Nicholl and Bill Lacey.

Burnley were Liverpool's opponents in the Final and for the first time a reigning monarch, George v, graced the occasion, sporting a red rose in his buttonhole. The crowd dropped to 72,000 for what was an 'unfashionable' Final and with the pitch hard and dusty the match was far from a classic. Injuries forced Liverpool to play without Harry Lowe, McKinlay coming in, but Burnley's loss was the greater for they had to replace their great goalkeeper Jerry Dawson with a reserve. Nevertheless the Cup went to East Lancashire. Soon after half-time Bert Freeman, who had scored some superb goals for Everton in his career, timed a volley so well that Kenny Campbell hardly saw the ball. Liverpool came back furiously towards the end. Lacey nearly scored when he hit a defender while Sewell was out of his goal and Burnley's reserve 'keeper made three fine saves in the closing minutes. There was a golden lining to this defeat for Liverpool had collected more than £14,000 from their Cup run – remember admission in those days was six old pennies – so they could enter the war years with a handsome bank balance.

Despite the outbreak of war in August 1914 the Football League competition continued for one more season until suspended for the duration. It was an undistinguished season for Liverpool, one they would like to expunge from the records. They lost to Sheffield United in the Cup in the fourth round and finished fourteenth in the League. But the sensation of that season came on Good Friday at Old Trafford. Both clubs were still in some danger of relegation, United more so than Liverpool. While Manchester needed both points, Liverpool needed to boost their goal average. United won 2–0 while Liverpool wasted chance after chance, even missing a penalty. The rumours flew that the match had been 'fixed' for a betting coup. Eventually the FA ordered an investigation, interference was proved and the sentences were severe. Eight players were suspended *sine die*, four from each club. Liverpool lost Fairfoul, Sheldon, Miller and Pursell and among the United four was the former Liverpool player 'Knocker' West. After the game some of the suspensions were lifted but West was given 'life'. He had to wait until 1945, when he was sixty-two.

Sheldon and Miller were able to re-start with Liverpool on the resumption of League football in 1919 and with Campbell, Longworth and McKinlay behind them the team were in much better shape than most of their rivals, finishing fourth. They were helped by some intriguing newcomers – the tall, lean Dick Forshaw, later to make a greater name with Everton, Harry 'Smiler' Chambers, a Geordie with bow legs and cannonball shot who became an England regular, and the more elegant Tommy Bromilow, also an international and later manager of Leicester and Burnley. Tommy Miller was capped by Scotland, before leaving for Manchester United, and Liverpool were able to enter the promised 'land fit for heroes' in good heart and high anticipation of great days to come.

Elisha Scott in action against Chelsea, January 1922.

The great Charlie Buchan in action for Arsenal against Liverpool, 1926.

3

Elisha Scott's Stronghold

Post-war London had the Flappers, cocktail parties and the world of P. G. Wodehouse. New York had the hip flask, the Model T Ford, Paul Whiteman and Scott Fitzgerald. Liverpool had flat caps, dole queues, the pawnshop, the corner pub and two great football clubs.

Liverpool were fourth again in the second post-war season but the club's strength was impressive. Both goalkeepers for the Ireland–England match at Celtic Park, Belfast in 1920, Kenny Campbell and Elisha Scott, were Liverpool players. Two locally born brothers, centre-half Walter Wadsworth and outside-left Harold Wadsworth had appeared and by 1922 there were four international full-backs at Anfield – Eph Longworth and Tommy Lucas (England), Don McKinlay (Scotland) and Ted Parry (Wales). So a team was taking shape: the great Scott in goal, the choice of four international-class backs, a middle line of Jock McNab, Wadsworth and Bromilow, with goals to come from Chambers and Forshaw.

A 3–0 defeat to an excellent Sunderland team at Roker was a disappointing start to 1922–3 but seven of the next fourteen matches were won and it was clear that Liverpool's massive defence would be difficult to overcome. A 3–1 defeat at Preston prefaced another fifteen games without defeat and if Chambers was leading scorer with only nineteen goals the defence conceded only thirty-six in forty-two matches. There was a stutter at the end, Liverpool taking only seven points from the last seven matches, but Spurs were unable to overtake them and the championship went to Anfield for a third time; the public, desperately hard up as they were, still topping 45,000 twice in the season.

Tommy Bromilow hugs the club mascot in the days when Liverpool needed luck.

Walter Wadsworth (*right*) shakes hands with the Southampton captain, FA Cup
third round, Southampton, 1924.

If their title was in dispute in 1922 Liverpool shattered all claims the following season, sweeping to the championship again with sixty points (the then record held by West Bromwich), six points clear of runners-up Sunderland. They lost only once at home, led the table throughout, conceded only thirty-one goals and took twenty-three points from twenty-one away games, figures that even Bill Shankly would respect. Between 30 December 1922 and 3 March 1923 Liverpool played eight First Division matches (Chelsea, Middlesbrough and West Bromwich twice, Blackburn and Bolton both at Anfield) without conceding a goal, such was Elisha Scott's stronghold. Darlington-born Fred Hopkins, Liverpool's outside-left in 325 League matches, scored his first and most famous goal (of a career total of nine!) in this season. 'Kneeler', a nickname derived from his habit of going down on one knee to cross the ball, put the ball in the net against Bolton, then on their way to the White Horse Final, and such was the shock to the firmament that the Kemlyn Road Stand caught fire. Dick Johnson (thirteen goals) joined the team to give support in attack to Chambers and Forshaw and any doubts about the efficiency of the forward line were swept away in a delirious first five home games in which twenty-three goals were scored, Everton going down 5–1.

This brilliant spell of two years was, in fact, the legacy of the great Tom Watson who, on his death in 1920, had bequeathed most of the double champions to a new manager David Ashworth. Despite this success Ashworth remained only two years at Anfield, leaving for Oldham Athletic and passing his managerial chair to a former player, a club founder in fact, Matt McQueen, one of McKenna's original recruits in 1892. He served the club as player, director and manager (apart from a spell as a League referee) until February 1928. Even the amputation of a leg in 1924 failed to dampen his enthusiasm for he still returned to manage the club for another four years. John McKenna had stepped down from the chair in 1919, W. R. Williams taking over, so a new regime had taken charge of a team at its peak and Liverpool entered a new era, the Jazz Age, full of enthusiasm. It might have developed into a golden age, for Liverpool continued to find splendid players and field fine teams, but what they failed to do, through the years of Depression and up to the Second World War, was to win another trophy. The glory crossed Stanley Park to Everton.

Curiously, despite Everton's glittering successes from 1927 to 1939, three First Division championships, the Cup and the Second Division

Fred Hopkins: a goal that set the stand on fire.

Jimmy 'Parson' Jackson (*right*) at Highbury, 1926.

Gordon Hodgson (*left*) with South African team-mate. His record of 233 League goals stood for years.

championship, Liverpool finished above them in eleven of the nineteen seasons. Scott's stronghold remained but Liverpool found it increasingly difficult to score goals and perhaps it was this frustration that led to a black day in Liverpool's history, 14 February 1925, when both Walter Wadsworth and McNab were sent off against Newcastle at Anfield. In the whole inter-war period Liverpool recorded only six dismissals.

New names in the twenty-year inter-war period brought an unusual sequence: Elisha Scott was English, Bob Ireland was a Scot, Sam English was Irish and George Poland was Welsh. It seemed only right and proper that Don Welsh, a Mancunian, should manage the club in due time. From 1929 the best League position Liverpool achieved was seventh and their Cup record was no more spectacular, reaching the last eight in 1920, 1924, 1925 and 1932. Significant arrivals in 1926 were Jimmy 'Parson' Jackson and Gordon Hodgson. Jackson, Newcastle born, joined Liverpool from Aberdeen and became a fine full-back or centre-half. He studied for the ministry and was ordained in 1933, one of only three Football League players to become clergymen since 1918. Hodgson decided to stay in Liverpool after touring England with a South African team, a decision that was to bring Liverpool 233 goals in 358 League matches, a record that stood until Roger Hunt surpassed it. Hodgson, with sixteen goals in 1926–7, arrived in time to allow Forshaw to move to Everton, a sensational move at the time, especially as he joined a title-winning team.

The following season saw the passing of another stalwart. McKinlay, injured at Villa Park, decided, as captain, to pull back inside-forward Jimmy McDougall to left-half. This inspired switch gave Liverpool an automatic selection for ten years and brought McDougall the leadership of Scotland. 'Smiler' Chambers had gone, too, moving to West Bromwich. Spion Kop was rebuilt in the familiar form of today, in 1929, and a succession of Scots (Tommy Reid from Motherwell, Jimmy Smith from Ayr) were brought in to help Hodgson's goal scoring. Hodgson's success set a trend at Anfield for in the period 1925–36 another eight South Africans were recruited. Arthur Riley became Scott's deputy and Berry Nieuwenheys was to adorn the left-wing from the mid-thirties, a tall slim player with a good shot. Liverpool began the new decade with a startling signing, paying £8,000, then the fourth highest fee in history, for Tom 'Tiny' Bradshaw of Bury. Bradshaw, one of Scotland's 1928 'Wembley Wizards', was taller than Ron Yeats, hence the nickname, but was also according to a contemporary writer, 'as dainty as a ballroom

A visit to the Mansion House –
Liverpool meet the Lord Mayor
of London, December 1927.

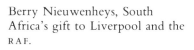

Berry Nieuwenheys, South
Africa's gift to Liverpool and the
RAF.

'Tiny' Bradshaw in 1936. His transfer fee of £8,000 was the fourth highest in history.

Tommy Cooper and Tommy Bradshaw keep an eye on a Charlton forward, 1936.
Hobson is the keeper.

dancer'. 'Tiny' 's arrival in Liverpool's defence saw the retirement of Tom Bromilow.

In 1932 came the first Cup clash with Everton since 1911. The third-round match, at Goodison, watched by 57,000, had a sensational start with Dean scoring off a post in twenty seconds. Despite that horrific start Bradshaw then policed Dean so well that Liverpool eventually won 2–1, the 'Parson', now Liverpool's captain, playing so splendidly the game was for ever remembered as 'Jackson's Match'. Harold Barton scored four in a 7–4 defeat of Everton's eventual Cupwinners at Anfield in 1933.

The much-heralded Rangers centre-forward English joined Liverpool later that year, but stayed only briefly after scoring eighteen goals in twenty-eight games.

A new chairman, Will Harrop, took office in 1935 as Elisha Scott's career closed. Eighty-eight goals had been conceded that season and the defence had to be strengthened. Liverpool went for the best, Tommy Cooper from Derby County and Ernie Blenkinsop from Sheffield Wednesday, the two England full-backs. Cooper was quick and a beautiful kicker of the ball. Blenkinsop positioned perfectly and the pair formed a marvellously balanced partnership, one of the best in history. Yet despite the indefatigable Hodgson, Liverpool were still unable to maintain a challenge to the giants of the time, Everton, Manchester City, a declining Huddersfield, a rising Arsenal. Another attempt to support Hodgson came with the signing of the distinguished Tommy 'Tosh' Johnson in 1935. 'Tosh' from Barrow, had made his name with Manchester City, but won his caps and medals in the Everton forward line of Dean and Jimmy Dunn. In fact he played only thirty-six matches for Liverpool, scoring eight times, and by the following season the great Gordon Hodgson had gone too, to Aston Villa for £4,000, after eleven seasons at Anfield and the feeling, perhaps, of flogging a dead horse.

By 1936 Liverpool had a fine defence again, but new manager George Kay, West Ham's captain in the 1923 Final, was left the task of building an attack that would encourage the many thousands of loyal Anfielders. Everton had seen too much of the sun. Fred Howe, from Stockport, had succeeded Hodgson as chief striker and a new and interesting forward was Jack Balmer, once an amateur with Everton, who began a long career by scoring eight goals in 1935–6. A skilful wing-half, Matt Busby, was signed from Manchester City, to form with Bradshaw and McDougall a Scotland half-back line, while Harry Eastham, one of the three brilliant

Ernie Blenkinsop (*left*), before his Liverpool days, playing for England against
Spain.

ball players in that family, improved the team's entertainment value if not the penetration. George Kay tried again. Ted Harston, fifty-five goals with Mansfield, was brought in but managed only five games for the First Division side. Willie Fagan, a nineteen-year-old from Preston, adapted much more successfully. So, too, did Phil Taylor, a youngster from Bristol Rovers and, as football was suspended in the beautiful but shadowed September of 1939, a burly centre-forward from Bootle, Cyril Done scored his first goal.

'Honest John' McKenna had died in 1936, loaded with honours. President of the Football League for twenty-six years, a vice-president of the FA, both secretary and chairman of the Liverpool club, his contribution to Anfield was rightly recognised by a plaque that catches the eye of all visitors. McKenna, the man who sent for the Scots, would have been the man above all to appreciate and savour the successes achieved by his beloved club after the war.

George Kay, Liverpool manager for fifteen years.

Jack Balmer, a deadly finisher who was the first player to score a hat-trick in three successive matches.

4

The green, green grass that Liddell used to play on

Cyril Done stood six feet tall, weighed thirteen stone and had the kick of a mule. Balmer was shrewd, skilful and delighted in beating a man before he could score. In April 1939 Liverpool signed professional a seventeen-year-old Scot who had joined them two years previously from Lochgelly Violet – Billy Liddell. An attack to win a championship was taking shape and Liddell was an outside-left shaped in heaven. If he were to re-appear today (November 1977) in Lochgelly it is not too fanciful to assume that an Italian, Spanish, or possibly American, club would pay £1,000,000 for him. In his early days at Anfield he survived a bad knee injury but as he gained strength and weight he emerged as a player of phenomenal acceleration, strength, shooting power, versatility and courage. 'The Flying Scot', one of his many appellations, was perhaps the most appropriate, for Billy did not beat defences; he roared through them like one of the great, gleaming pre-war steam trains, racing through country wayside stations. And such was his chivalry that no defenders ever bore him malice and tried to hack him down. They were happy, like those country stationmasters, to bask in the reflected glow of such power and speed. Billy had a computerised left foot that could float across centres or – a tactical variation he virtually copyrighted – hit them hard and low. He had a right foot like the hammer of Thor.

George Kay had to promise Billy's parents when he signed him up that he would be allowed to continue a career in accountancy. Billy qualified, served in the RAF, became a lay preacher and JP and performed wonders among Liverpool's kids. He was capped by Scotland in a wartime

47

Cyril Done, a
thirteen-stone regular
scorer.

Billy Liddell lets fly – against Burnley, April 1950. An early knee injury did little
to prevent his pulverising the opponents' defence.

Cyril Sidlow, Bob Paisley, Ray Lambert and Phil Taylor.

international in 1942 (his contemporaries that day included Shankly, Busby, Dodds, Lawton, Mercer and Hagan), but he made his first real impact in his second match for Liverpool. He scored three against the legendary Frank Swift and Manchester City in a 7–1 wartime league win.

Liddell, still in the RAF, missed Liverpool's re-introduction to peacetime football, an inspired tour of Canada and the USA. George Kay theorised that North American sunshine, orange juice and thick steaks were the best preparation for the First Division and he may well have been right. Liverpool returned having gained, on average, seven pounds each, and the stamina and impetus gained took them to their fourth championship.

Busby had rejected an offer to coach Liverpool, to become manager of hard-up, blitzed Manchester United. Tommy Cooper, an Army despatch rider, had been killed in the war. Cyril Sidlow, a six-foot Welshman, had been signed from Wolves to keep goal and played for his country. So, too, did Phil Taylor at wing-half and when Neil Franklin left Stoke and England for Bogota, Liverpool's new centre-half Laurie Hughes, from Tranmere, took over in the national side. Another newcomer to win an England cap was Bill Jones who could play in most positions, but is remembered as a centre-half, while Eddie Spicer, a schoolboy international, was developing into one of the best left-backs in the club's history when the second of two broken legs ended his career prematurely.

It was in their second home match of that 1946–7 season against Chelsea and the newly signed Tommy Lawton, that Liverpool warned football of their new power. They led 4–0 at half-time, 6–0 after fifty minutes, were then hit by a whirlwind Chelsea counter-attack that brought the score back to 6–4, before Balmer made it seven! Years of blackouts and rationing and the new austerity were forgotten in that delirious ninety minutes. The red half of Merseyside came to earth with a bump, for in Liverpool's next match, away to Matt Busby's new United, they crashed 5–0. The reaction was spectacular.

Liverpool had a new chairman, Billy McConnell, principal of a catering firm, who had taken office in 1944. He knew that Everton's manager Theo Kelly was anxious to sign the new star in the North East, the tall, slim, red-haired Newcastle centre-forward Albert Stubbins. When McConnell heard that Everton were about to move he went to Goodison Park for a midweek game, slipped away at half-time and drove straight to Newcastle. His offer of £12,000, then a record fee, was accepted and when Kelly arrived the following morning the deal had been all but completed.

Chairman Billy McConnell.

Newcastle had been flashing messages on cinema screens to get Stubbins to St James's Park. Kelly's bid was £12,500 but Albert told him: 'I have already promised to sign for Liverpool and I never go back on my word.' Stubbins's introduction into George Kay's team, with Liddell, Balmer, Done and Fagan all available for support, clinched the championship that season in the face of intense rivalry from the newly risen Manchester United and a highly accomplished Stoke team. Stubbins, who won only one England cap, such was the intense competition at the time, scored in a 3–1 win at Bolton, the start of a run of twelve games without defeat.

November 1946 belonged to Jackie Balmer. No player had ever scored hat-tricks in three successive matches and that is what Balmer achieved in that month: three against Portsmouth on 9 November, four against Derby at the Baseball Ground on the 16th and another three against Arsenal on 23 November. A reminder that the defence could have its less responsible days came when Wolves visited Anfield and won 5–1, Denis Westcott scoring four. The onset of that cruel winter of 1946–7 saw the departure of Nieuwenheys and Eastham, Fagan spending a while on the flank. Stubbins scored three in a memorable Cup-tie against Birmingham, one immortalised as 'the goal in the snow'. Liddell fired in a hard, low free kick and Stubbins, with the score 1–1, launched himself head first across the snow and ice to score with a brilliant header.

The backlog of unplayed matches accumulated during the appalling weather. As conditions eased Cup-ties were given precedence over League games and Liverpool reached the semi-final, to become favourites to take the FA Cup. Alan Brown's iron Burnley blocked the way to Wembley and a late goal by Ray Harrison meant that Liverpool had to turn their attention back to the League. Bobby Paisley, a tough little wing-half from Hetton le Hole, Durham, had forced his way into the team, and he still remembers that astonishing finish to the season – in June. Liverpool had seven matches to play, only two at home, but were nine points behind Wolves. Bob recalls: 'Wolves picked up one more point from seven matches. We took thirteen of our last fourteen points, but even then Stoke would have won the championship if they had won their last match at Sheffield United.' Manchester United finished on fifty-six, Wolves also had fifty-six and Liverpool, whose last match was at Wolves, had fifty-five. It was Stan Cullis's last match, too, so Molineux was a place for strong hearts. Liverpool's 2–1 win that day was deserving of the championship. Wolves attacked furiously throughout, Sidlow performed magnificently,

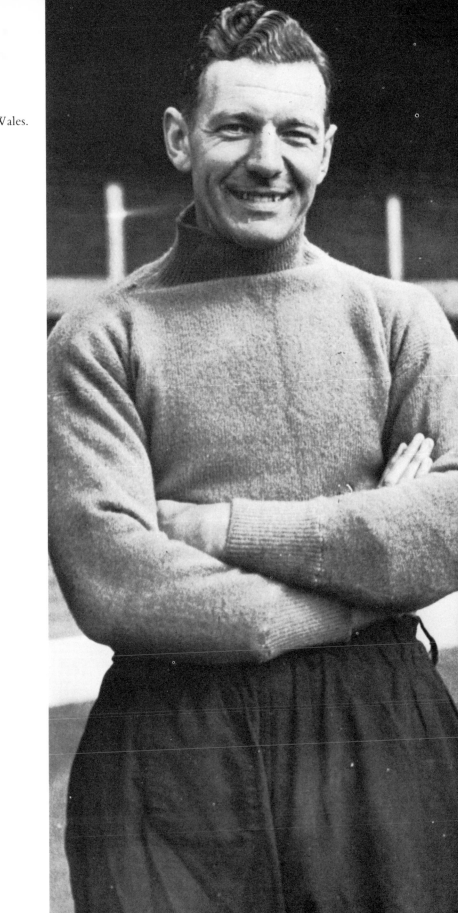

Cyril Sidlow,
Liverpool and Wales.

Liddell had to drop back to defence and Liverpool won by breakaway goals from Balmer and Stubbins. Another fortnight was to pass before Stoke's last game at Sheffield – they could win on goal average. Liverpool beat Everton at Anfield that day, 2–1 in the Final of the Liverpool Senior Cup, but the nerve ends stretched to Sheffield and Bramall Lane. Said Bob: 'No one dared go home. We all sat around, waiting, waiting till at last we got the final score – Sheffield United 2, Stoke City 1. We were the champions!'

A vicious winter was followed by the golden summer of 1947, the year of Compton and Edrich and runs galore. Anfield was a happy spot, the championship won, Balmer and Stubbins had each scored twenty-four goals, Done ten, Fagan and Liddell seven each and Billy had been chosen to play for Great Britain against the Rest of Europe. Along with Paisley, a staunch new full-back had arrived, Ray Lambert, signed while at school as a thirteen-year-old and soon to become a Welsh international. Liverpool's average attendance had soared to 45,000 and trying to get into the first team were Spicer, South African Bob Priday, Done, and full-back Jim Harley, quick enough to have won the Powderhall Sprint (under the pseudonym of A. B. Mitchell) as an eighteen-year-old.

Yet the next season was a comparative failure, Liverpool dropping to eleventh place, and the only explanation can be in the tremendous all-round improvement among First Division rivals. There were probably enough great and good players in the country in 1948 to have raised four England teams. Stubbins, who joined Liddell in the Kop's pantheon, hit twenty-six goals that season, including four in one game against Huddersfield, but Anfielders' favourite memory was the double over Everton – 3–0 at Anfield, 4–0 at Goodison! There was also a memorable occasion on 14 February 1948 when 44,840 spectators crowded St James's Park, Newcastle, for a friendly match. Liverpool were the visitors, Stubbins was making his first return to Tyneside since his transfer and the attendance remains a record for a friendly. Attractive and star-studded as they were Liverpool were unable to capitalise on that first post-war championship. Jimmy Payne, a winger whose speed and dribbling skills evoked comparisons with Matthews and Finney, was a brief but brilliant meteor in those years. Liddell, heading a goal against Portsmouth from outside the penalty area, and Stubbins (against Middlesbrough he pulled down a headed pass from Paisley and scored from twenty-five yards) continued their spectacular careers and the club was graced with talent in other posi-

The grin that captured Anfield – Albert Stubbins and wife.

Albert Stubbins opens fire, 1949.

Determination – the name of Bill Jones's game.

Eddie Spicer and Willie Fagan, 1949.

tions but not until 1950 did Liverpool once again show signs of getting to the top.

This time Liverpool reached their second FA Cup Final and their first appearance at Wembley. Their defence had been proved in a League run of nineteen matches without defeat, even though Balmer and full-back Bill Shepherd, who had succeeded Harley, dropped out after a rough match with Stoke. Kevin Baron, who had been waiting four years in the Central League, formed a new inside-forward partnership with Fagan. Lambert, switching over, struck up a full-back partnership with Spicer, Taylor replaced Balmer as captain, Liddell was available all along the forward line and Done was always a willing deputy for the heavily marked and frequently injured Stubbins. Liverpool's Cup run began with a lucky third-round victory over Second Division Blackburn. If the Rovers had been able to finish they would have won at Ewood. At Anfield Liverpool got home 2–1, but only after the Blackburn outside-left had failed to score with a shot that hit both posts! Victories over Exeter City and Stockport County, after a stern struggle, took Liverpool to the last eight, a home tie against the Blackpool of Matthews and Mortensen. At last Liverpool began to show some form, again winning 2–1 the winning goal coming from a now regular tactical switch, Payne to the left, Liddell to the right.

The semi-final was a historic day on Merseyside – The Grand National at Aintree and Liverpool v Everton at Maine Road, Manchester. In fact the match wasn't big enough for the occasion, Liverpool winning comfortably 2–0. Liddell, chasing a chip into the box from Paisley, roared in with such speed and power that Everton's 'keeper George Burnett fumbled and the ball bounced in over the line. In the second half another Everton panic, an attempt to concede a corner, gave Liverpool possession and Liddell, even when faced with a narrow angle, was deadly in those situations.

The Wembley opponents were Tom Whittaker's powerful Arsenal, a team that most critics would regard as the club's best post-war team despite the record of the 1970–1 side: George Swindin, Laurie Scott, Wally Barnes, Alex Forbes, Leslie Compton, Joe Mercer, Jimmy Logie, Reg Lewis, Denis Compton – players of the class of Archie Macaulay, Don Roper and Lionel Smith were kept waiting in the reserves. Liverpool approached Wembley with three successive League victories and faced an Arsenal who had lost three of their seven games after their replayed semi-final with Chelsea. Were Arsenal, acknowledged as long in the tooth, running out of wind? A more immediate question was that of

The Cup that Liverpool missed, 1950 – Joe Mercer, Arsenal captain, has a firm hold.

Arsenal's captain Joe Mercer, transferred by Everton in 1946, who had never left his Hoylake home and had done all his midweek training with the Liverpool staff at Anfield. Clearly the most generous of hosts could not allow a Cup Final opponent access to Wembley planning and Joe had to do his training alone in the afternoons.

Liverpool stayed at Weybridge over night on the Friday, Arsenal had lunch at their own ground instead of the Great Northern, such were the preparations. Manager George Kay travelled with Liverpool, but was far from well. The midweek snow in late April 1950 had given way to rain and both camps were happy with the thought of a heavy pitch. Both teams had to change, Liverpool to white shirts with red facings, black shorts and black and white hooped stockings; Arsenal to old-gold shirts, white shorts, black and gold hooped stockings. Again, for Liverpool, it was a Royal Final, and the teams were presented to George VI. Laurie Hughes, fit again, returned to the side at centre-half and with Bill Jones playing so well the unlucky man to drop out was Bobby Paisley. Kevin Baron, conversely, kept his place although Jack Balmer was also fit again, and in the inquests to follow these two selection decisions were heavily criticised. So the team for the Final read: Sidlow, Lambert, Spicer, Taylor, Hughes, Jones, Payne, Baron, Stubbins, Fagan, Liddell.

Arsenal scored in the seventeenth minute and from then onwards Liverpool could never quite catch them. Leslie Compton, heading out of defence, saw Barnes deliver a long, accurate pass to Logie. As Liverpool re-grouped Peter Goring, the obvious recipient of Logie's pass, darted off to the left taking Hughes with him and Logie was able to slide the ball through to Lewis, stealing in on the right side. Sidlow was left defenceless and Lewis was too experienced to miss such a chance, neatly pushing the ball past Sidlow's left hand from twelve yards. Liddell, the most marked man in the Liverpool team, had to take some heavy tackling from Forbes and Scott, but true to character, refused to complain afterwards: 'Though the game was a hard one I thought at the time, and still do, that it was perfectly fair.' Liverpool's best chance came three minutes after the interval. Liddell's high, fierce cross was finger-tipped out by Swindin, Payne rushed in to head it into what appeared to be an empty net only to see the ball sail into Swindin's arms. The seventeenth minute of the second half was fatal. Cox, standing with his back to goal, flicked the ball first time past Spicer, and Lewis ran on to beat Sidlow's left hand yet again.

Liverpool had no complaints. Their defence was suspect, their mid-field uninspired and what appeared to be a brilliant attack was contained. Merseyside took a deep gulp of disappointment and stayed loyal. Thousands lined the streets waiting to greet their team's return and there were thousands more at Anfield and at the Town Hall. That day a Liverpool footballer could say, with absolute conviction: 'We have the best supporters in the land.'

That loyalty was to be severely tested in the next years, for Wembley 1950 was the crest of the wave for the first post-war champions. George Kay's fifteen-year reign as Liverpool's manager ended in 1951 through ill-health. For his successor the club turned to Don Welsh, a famous Charlton forward who was Manchester born and who had become an Anfield favourite while a wartime guest player. Welsh had wanted to join Liverpool as a coach, but Charlton had refused to release him. Now he came in full charge to inherit a still-stable defence but a fast-fading attack.

Stubbins scored only six times in twenty-three League games in 1950-1. Baron, Fagan and Balmer all lost form and it was left to the still-magnificent Liddell to carry the scoring responsibilities. The strains up front led, inevitably, to extra pressure on the rear. Sidlow, conceding four goals in ten minutes to Newcastle at Anfield, was replaced and a defence that had missed Hughes, who had been absent from the side all season after an injury in the Charity Shield, was also looking shaky by 1952. A short summer tour of Sweden brought another blow when Spicer broke a leg and 1951-2 saw a team disintegrating. Taylor and Hughes missed half the season with knee trouble, Stubbins needed a thigh operation. Charlie Ashcroft had settled in goal (winning a selection for England 'B') and Jones at full-back, so despite all the problems Liverpool did manage to finish a respectable eleventh. In retrospect perhaps it would have been better for the long-term future had the results been worse. For this was a false recovery and the weaknesses in the first-team structure were papered over, bringing, inevitably, the crash of 1954. A fourth-round Cup-tie against Wolves, then England's leading team, attracted a 61,000 crowd to Anfield but the run ended with a 2-0 defeat in the fifth round at Burnley, Les Shannon, once a Liverpool player, contributing greatly to that victory.

By 1952-3 all the signs were ominous. The League was one long struggle, culminating in an escape from relegation in the last match, Chelsea being deafened to a 2-0 defeat by an anxious Anfield crowd. Perhaps

Kevin Baron, about to shoot
against Burnley.

Don Welsh, in managerial pose.

Geoff Twentyman, waiting for his chance.

John Molyneux, Bert Slater and Louis Bimpson.

Ronnie Moran, winning the ball, as usual.

Billy Liddell, twice a Great Britain player.

even more ignominious was a 1–0 Cup defeat at Gateshead, then a Third Division club. The pitch was mud-covered – several players claimed it was the worst they had ever seen – while spectators said it was impossible to see clearly because of the fog! Such was Liverpool's desperation the valiant Jones was switched into attack. Stubbins playing only four times in his farewell season. A big, willing centre-forward from Burscough, Louis Bimpson made his début and other promising newcomers were Alan A'Court, an outside-left from Prescot and a strong full-back, Ronnie Moran, signed on the recommendation of a friend of the director, T. V. Williams. Liverpool also paid out their first big fee (£12,000) for a long time when they took Sammy Smyth, a skilful Irish international who first made his name with Wolves, from Stoke. But Sammy's best days were behind him and he played only forty-four games before retiring.

It was clear, from the very start of the 1953–4 term, that Liverpool were in trouble. All the first fourteen away games were lost and some of the defeats were alarming – 5–1 at Old Trafford, 6–0 at Charlton, 5–1 at Portsmouth, 5–2 at Chelsea and West Bromwich. Spicer broke his leg, for a second·time, the end of his career and so catastrophic were the results that the mighty Liddell was switched to full-back. There were more signings – goalkeeper Dave Underwood from Watford, centre-half Geoff Twentyman from Carlisle, to be followed, on Christmas Day, by two signings from Don Welsh's old club Charlton, full-back Frank Lock and forward John Evans. Then came another full-back, Tom McNulty from Manchester United. Bimpson scored four goals in a 4–0 rout of Burnley and Smyth twice in a 6–1 defeat of Villa. But only nine matches were won and with twenty-eight points Liverpool finished two behind the twenty-first club Middlesbrough and were back in the Second Division for the first time since 1905.

'Straight back' was the campaign theme for 1954–5 and with Billy Liddell now at centre-forward and hitting thirty goals (out of ninety-two, the club's highest total since 1905) and Evans adding another twenty-nine, including four against Bristol Rovers, the attack was clearly good enough to shoot Liverpool back into the senior class. But sadly the defence was no better than in the relegation season, although Twentyman settled into a hard but constructive wing-half, a player who, with a little more pace, would have been capped frequently. The good cheer of another disappointing season came in the Cup. Everton, winning promotion, had passed Liverpool when they were on the way down the previous spring

Three internationals: Alan A'Court and Laurie Hughes (England), Billy Liddell (Scotland).

and were the premier club when the rivals met in the fourth round at Goodison. As Liverpool had lost ten and drawn two of their previous twelve away games there could be, felt Evertonians, only one result to this tie.

By half-time the score was 2–0 to Liverpool and Goodison was wearing a deeper shade of blue. Liddell (who else?) had side-stepped a tackle in the box to score first and A'Court added a second while Everton were still girding themselves. Hughes had more knee trouble in the second half, Liddell had to drop back to midfield but Twentyman performed magnificently against the fiery Dave Hickson. Then Evans completed a superb day for Anfield with two late goals. Much anguish was washed away that afternoon.

Liddell played a second time for Great Britain before the 1955–6 season, he and Stanley Matthews being the only survivors from the Great Britain team of eight years before. It was Liddell, again, in that season who scored a famous 'extra time' goal. Liverpool had drawn with Manchester City, the eventual Cupwinners, in the fifth-round tie at Maine Road. City were leading 2–1 in the replay when Liddell broke through magnificently across the snow, beat the mighty Trautmann with a ferocious shot, and then found that the last whistle had gone a second previously.

During this season John Molyneux, from Chester, replaced Ray Lambert (308 League matches) at full-back; Dick White, from Scunthorpe, appeared at centre-half and Jimmy Melia, a skilful ball player, arrived from St Anthony's School.

John Evans had a famous day.

Dick White and Jimmy Melia.

5

The December Earthquake

It is difficult in the late 1970s to recall the frustration around Anfield twenty years ago. The support was loyal and intense, the club had talented players, the whole ambience was First Division and yet, season after season, Liverpool always expired just below the summit. After their eleventh position in 1954–5 their placings in the Second Division were 3, 3, 4, 4, 3, 3. The Board, it should be said, did at least have patience but Don Welsh paid the price towards the end of the 1955–6 season when he was replaced by the club coach Phil Taylor.

Liddell, switching from right-wing to centre-forward as the occasion demanded, still wore the purple and had strong support from Arnell and A'Court with Johnny Wheeler, a strong and adaptable attacking midfielder from Bolton, arriving in 1956–7. Another exciting reinforcement came from Scotland, Tommy Younger, a Scottish international goalkeeper from Hibernian. Younger's height and strength meant that Liverpool could at least claim the best defence in the Second Division. Phil Taylor finished his first season with a flourish, seven wins and two draws in the last ten matches, but Liverpool were always liable to drop the vital point. A'Court was capped by England, Younger by Scotland, Moran played for the League and Gerry Byrne made his début at left-back – and put through his own goal. There were more signings for 1957–8 – winger Tony McNamara from Everton, inside-forward Jimmy Harrower from Hibernian. Liddell passed Elisha Scott's record of 429 League games and Anfield's floodlights were turned on on 30 October.

A poor start, ten points from the first eleven games, wrecked hopes in

Alan Arnell, Barry Wilkinson and Jimmy Melia.

Johnny Wheeler, the
strong man from
Bolton.

Tommy Younger, the sometimes brilliant Scottish goalkeeper.

1958–9 and one match that must have left a deep impression in the Anfield boardroom was a 5–0 hiding at Huddersfield where Town were managed by Bill Shankly. Fred Morris, a big strong winger from Mansfield, was recruited, the great Liddell was dropped for the first time and Bimpson and Arnell were the new spearheads. Melia and Harrower were perhaps too much alike in style to be complementary. Once again it was clear, despite their ability, Liverpool were not a good enough team. A Cup defeat by Southern League club Worcester City – Liddell was twelfth man and helped stud the boots – was the nadir. Liddell was recalled on Good Friday 1959, at the age of thirty-seven, to score twice against Barnsley – and hit the bar – and went on to score fourteen goals in nineteen more appearances, a record that made his five months' absence all the more mysterious. Younger became player-manager of Falkirk that summer, Bert Slater, part of the transfer deal, taking his place for a spell in Liverpool's goal. A surprising signing, that of centre-forward Dave Hickson from Everton, for £12,000 in November 1959, was the prelude to a new era at Anfield. On 17 November Phil Taylor resigned, admitting: 'I'm tired. The strain of trying to win promotion has proved too much.'

The last time Liverpool directors had seen Bill Shankly was during that 5–0 drubbing at Huddersfield. They left Leeds Road, said Shankly afterwards, 'in single file, with their shoulders slumped, like a funeral procession'. Chairman T. V. Williams and director Harry Latham went to see Shankly while Huddersfield were playing Cardiff. 'How would you like to manage the best club in the country?' was the question put to Shankly. 'Why, is Matt Busby packing up?' he countered. His caution was justified. In 1951, when Shankly was manager at Carlisle, he had received a call from Liverpool asking him to attend an interview for the purpose of replacing George Kay, who had just resigned. In the course of his journey, back and forth, he saw two other candidates, Andy Beattie and Scot Symon. He discussed the job with Beattie and both knew they had failed to get the job which, of course, went to Don Welsh. Allowing for Shankly's disappointment, his recollection of the episode gives a strong clue to the difficulties of managing Liverpool in that era: 'The big snag had cropped up when the Liverpool board had said the manager could put down his team for matches and the directors would scrutinise it and alter it if they wanted too. So I said, "If I don't pick the team, what am I manager of?"'

Not until December 1959 did Shankly agree to take over and when

75

Dave Hickson, stormy petrel.

Perfect balance: Ian Callaghan made his début in 1960.

he arrived he hit the club like an earthquake. Anfield, he decided, was 'an eyesore'; Melwood, the training ground, 'a wilderness, but there was space'. There were no facilities for watering Anfield so he insisted on spending £3,000. Within a month he had drawn up a list of twenty-four players to be released and they had all gone within a year. Shankly absolved both Don Welsh and Phil Taylor from some of the blame for the years of mediocrity when he wrote: 'It is difficult to believe how hard I had to fight to make certain people realise the potential of the club. They had been so unsuccessful that they were pessimistic, frightened to do anything. They had got into a position where they were scared, like gamblers, on a losing streak who were afraid to bet any more'. Complacency was another foe. 'Some directors thought the club was all right. They were in the top half of the Second Division and getting crowds of 24,000.'

His first move was to try to sign up Jack Charlton, the Leeds centre-half who was to become an England World Cupwinner in 1966. 'We offered £18,000 for him. Leeds wanted more, not a lot more, but more than our people felt they could afford.' So he turned to Scotland. While at Huddersfield he had watched two young players, Ian St John, the Motherwell centre-forward, and Ron Yeats, a centre-half of Dundee United, but Huddersfield could afford neither. Shankly decided that he could never get the Liverpool team right until he strengthened them down the middle. The problem was one of persuasion. Could he convince the Board that around £70,000 would be needed to sign these two twenty-three-year-old players?

After Shankly's arrival Liverpool had finished third, again just missing promotion after scoring ninety goals. Ian Callaghan, a seventeen-year-old outside-right, made his début in April 1960. Roger Hunt, twenty-one, a strong forward from the Warrington area, was the success of the season with twenty-one League and Cup goals, while the gap left by Twenty-man's departure to Ballymena was filled by a Scottish signing, Tommy Leishman from Hibernian.

In Shankly's first full season, 1960–1, the team began taking shape. Gordon Milne, son of Shankly's old Preston colleague Jimmy Milne, was signed for £12,000. Gerry Byrne was taken off the transfer list and, after exposure to Shankly's evangelism, replaced Ronnie Moran at left-back, rapidly becoming one of the best defenders in England. Sheffield United supplied Kevin Lewis, a strong-running winger, yet one of Shankly's major moves received hardly any attention. It is the custom of most

Gordon Milne, the son of Jimmy, Shankly's colleague at Preston.

The Spearhead – Roger Hunt as the new lad in the dressing-room ... and as a
World Cupwinner.

Ian St John – 'The Saint' – comes to Liverpool.

Ronnie Yeats – 'The Colossus'.

managers, on moving into office, to change the coaching and training staff. Shankly told Bob Paisley, Reuben Bennett and Joe Fagan that he had full confidence in them and in that one small speech he did more for Liverpool's future than several six-figure signings.

He had less confidence in his team and he still hankered after those two Scots, Yeats and St John. Eventually the Board, after seeing Liverpool finish third yet again in 1960–1, backed Shankly's judgement. Bill gives the credit to a new director, Eric Sawyer, a powerful figure in the Littlewood's organisation. Alerted by a Scottish Sunday newspaper story that St John wanted a transfer, Shankly was in Motherwell on Monday evening to beat off a challenge from Newcastle United with a £37,500 fee. St John had been at Liverpool only a week when he scored three goals against Everton in the Liverpool Senior Cup, a feat that brought immediate canonisation. 'What would you do if Christ came to Liverpool?' asked a local church's notice board. 'Play St John at inside-left' was the Kop's reply, written underneath.

Yeats was signed at 4 pm on a Saturday afternoon in July, in Edinburgh, for a fee of £30,000 to Dundee United. Shankly told his directors: 'These players will not only win us promotion – they'll win us the Cup as well. I'll stake my life on it.' Not since 'Tiny' Bradshaw had Liverpool had a player of Yeats's height and strength. 'The Colossus', as Shankly admiringly called Yeats, and 'The Saint' arrived only just in time. The great Liddell had retired in September 1960, a crowd of 38,000 attending his benefit match, but even the Anfielders' patience was wearing thin and a season's average attendance of 29,000 suggested that even the faithful were doubtful about the team's future.

By 1961–2 Shankly had got it right. The promotion campaign was a triumphal march. The team dropped only one point in their first eleven matches (with a dazzling goal average of 31–4!) and in all won twenty-seven of their forty-two League matches. With sixty-two points they finished eight ahead of the second-placed club, Leyton, were unbeaten at home for the first time since the 1905 season, while the average gate shot up to 39,000, only Spurs and Everton topping those figures. Hunt rampaged among Second Division defences, scoring forty-one League goals to break Gordon Hodgson's club record and winning his first England cap. A'Court, Byrne, Melia and Milne played in all matches while Leishman, St John, Yeats and Hunt missed two or less. Callaghan replaced Lewis at outside-right midway through the season and Jim Furnell, a tall,

Jimmy Furnell had a brief but distinguished spell as Liverpool's goalkeeper.

strong 'keeper from Burnley took over from Slater. That season also saw the end of the maximum wage for players, a surrender by the Football League that must have brought a wry smile from the ghost of John McKenna, remembering his lost battle on that issue at the start of the century.

Unlimited money also meant, as far as Shankly and his lieutenants were concerned, unlimited work for the players. Melwood was turned into the best club training ground in the country and a training system was built up that ensured Liverpool would have the fittest players. Shankly has given examples. Hunt, taking an exercise in tight control involving use of the ball against boards placed fifteen yards apart, was ashen after forty-five seconds at his first attempt. He was later to continue for two minutes. Three-a-side games, played on a pitch forty-five yards long and twenty-five yards wide, were originally played five minutes each way. That was thought to be the players' limit. In successive seasons the games were lengthened until players could last thirty minutes each way. The training was hard and sustained but intelligently planned so that players never became bored. The European Cup was won in the sweat and strain of Melwood for it was there that the campaign to conquer the continent began.

It's mine! Few argued with Tommy Lawrence.

Ex-Ranger Willie Stevenson, a creative midfield player.

6

Your Raiment all Red

Back to the big league was a bumpy ride but Shankly and his lieutenants learned from the experience. Anfield's expectations of a continuation of the parade through Division II were shattered in the first three matches of 1962–3, Blackpool and Blackburn both inflicting home defeats, a point being scrambled from a 2–2 draw with Manchester City at Maine Road.

The first First Division derby for eleven years brought a 73,000 crowd to Goodison where Liverpool, without the injured St John, were happy with a 2–2 draw that brought them their ninth point from their first ten games.

Shankly believed Leicester to be the best team of that season ('the only team we learned anything from') and it was after a 3–0 defeat at Filbert Street that the next major change was made, Tommy Lawrence, a burly Scot who had spent five years in the reserves, superseding Furnell in goal. The change brought only another defeat so the following week Shankly and Paisley swooped on Rangers' Reserves and signed Willie Stevenson for £27,000. Stevenson, whose enormous creative gifts in midfield were to be appreciated only slowly, replaced the hard-working Leishman, yet the immediate consequence was another defeat, by Burnley. A 3–3 draw at Old Trafford on 10 November was the turning point. Lawrence and Stevenson settled in, the team found their feet and eleven of their next twelve League and Cup fixtures were won.

From late December came the great freeze lasting until March, bringing a huge backlog of fixtures. Yet the League momentum continued and it needed Leicester, with Banks performing brilliantly in goal, to break

Chris Lawler watches the young
Allan Clarke of Fulham.

Peter Thompson, a winger to
compare with Liddell and the
cutting edge Shankly needed to
win the championship.

the spell with a 2–0 win at Anfield. By Easter of this extraordinary season Liverpool had risen to sixth in the League table and had also reached the FA Cup semi-final. The League? The Cup? The Double?

Sadly, Easter was the high tide. Good Friday brought Spurs to Merseyside, not quite the brilliant team that had performed the double two years before, but still a very talented and at times glittering combination. By half-time, before a stunned Anfield, Spurs were leading 2–0. Stevenson, with a thunderbolt goal, gave the Kop hope and then, suddenly, Spurs crumbled and Melia (2), St John and Lewis turned impending defeat into an exhilarating 5–2 victory. St John's goal sank Manchester United on Easter Saturday and Liverpool went to White Hart Lane for the return with Spurs on the Monday and this time Tottenham had ample revenge. Greaves, at his best, scored four times, the final margin being 7–2 and a shattered Liverpool were unable to contain Nottingham Forest in mid-week. The championship had gone.

Liverpool went into the Cup semi-final at Hillsborough like avengers. Surely, this time, Leicester must fall. Try as they did, and Liverpool attacked furiously for most of the match, Leicester's style – they were the first successful 4–3–3 team in the First Division – proved unbreakable. A goal by Stringfellow, halfway through the first half, was sufficient. Leicester's successes that season – they won great praise but no trophies – set Shankly thinking. When Melia, an orthodox inside-forward, was injured Shankly had experimented with playing Chris Lawler as an additional centre-half alongside Yeats and pushed Milne forward. But only so far as to leave Liverpool able to adapt from 4–2–4 to 4–3–3 according to the situation. The numbers game had begun.

So a season of experiment may have ended in disappointment on the Kop, Liverpool finishing eighth in the First Division, but was one of considerable satisfaction for Shankly and Paisley. The club was re-established as a major power. A'Court, Milne, Hunt, Byrne and Melia had played for England, Lawrence and St John for Scotland and the payroll listed Callaghan, Yeats and Lawler, all future internationals. The shape of the game was changing but the object, to score goals, remained constant and when Liverpool summarised the season they realised that Hunt (twenty-four) and St John (nineteen) were their only consistent scorers. If progress was to continue then reinforcements were needed.

Liverpool paid £40,000 for Peter Thompson of Preston before the 1963–4 season started and with that one signing Shankly had the cutting

Gerry Byrne. Under Shankly's management he became one of the best defenders in the country.

edge he needed to win the championship. The Kop had already begun to adapt popular songs to express their own unrealised ambitions – 'the green, green grass that Liddell used to play on'. Now, with Thompson, they needed to mourn Liddell's retirement no longer. Here again was a left-winger of pace, power and explosive shooting.

Yet a season of change and distinction started slowly. The Kemlyn Road stand had been rebuilt and by 1964 the club's famous colours would be changed from red shirts and white shorts to an all-red strip, a costume that brought Macaulay's great lines to mind:

> Oh, wherefore come ye forth
> In triumph from the North
> With your hands and your feet
> And your raiment all red?

Nine points from nine games was followed by a 3–0 crash to Sheffield United at Bramall Lane yet Shankly refused to be alarmed into changes and his confidence was well placed. From Sheffield Liverpool swept on to the championship, taking forty-seven points from the next thirty games, starting with a 2–1 defeat of champions Everton and finishing with a rout of Arsenal at Anfield when Thompson hit two thunderous goals that sent the Kop into ecstasy. Alf Arrowsmith, a centre-forward in his own right, had now emerged as Hunt's deputy, even alternative, allowing Liverpool to adjust their formation once again, St John joining Milne in the midfield. Furnell had moved on to Arsenal and Melia joined Wolves, while in the Cup Liverpool attracted 42,000 to a fourth-round replay at Port Vale.

That Cup campaign is still a sour memory on Merseyside. Port Vale's effrontery in forcing a draw at Enfield was followed by a sixth-round home draw against Swansea, fifth from bottom of the Second Division. There were important psychological stresses. Liverpool, never having won the Cup and with a record of failure when within sight of the Final, were always nervous. Swansea were experiencing a sensational run of victories, full of confidence and possibly unaware of the dimensions of their task. Shankly was well versed in psychological warfare, and had a plaque bearing the Liver bird erected above the tunnel that leads from the dressing-rooms. The first time Malcolm Macdonald saw it he called to his manager, Newcastle's Joe Harvey: 'Well, you've got us to the right ground, boss.' Swansea's manager Trevor Morris said to his team, as they

The new Kemlyn Road stand.

Alf Arrowsmith, the aptly named
centre-forward.

trooped out on that historic day for South Wales: 'You're leaving here as boys. You'll come back as men....' Adding, as the door closed on the last man: 'If you come back at all.' They did return, crowned with laurels after one of the most stunning performances in FA Cup history, winning 2–1 mostly through an astonishing goalkeeping performance by Noel Dwyer, who even saved a penalty shot from Moran.

The Cup shock caused, not unnaturally, a stumble in the League and when Yeats was suspended, to miss the three Easter matches – one against those sinister blue men from Leicester – Anfield was apprehensive. There was no need for concern. The finishing academy at Melwood was now in full swing and Lawler, that imperturbable stripling, filled Yeats's centre-half place so impressively that all three games were won. Liverpool had thus won the Second and First Division championships in three seasons and this time, 1964, they could also look forward to campaigning in Europe for the first time.

Their success brought them another – their fourth – invitation for a summer tour of the United States. Liverpool, home of the Beatles, was then a fascinating city to most young Americans and Shankly's team received a huge welcome. They even received the accolade of appearing, with Gerry and the Pacemakers, on the Ed Sullivan Show from New York, a promotional feat by the *Daily Express*'s Derek Potter. Less encouraging was a knee injury to Yeats and the increasing pressures of a long tour, spent playing against teams always anxious to beat champions.

The tactical talkers, Joe Fagan and
Bob Paisley.

Eric Sawyer, the director who
made the figures add up for Bill
Shankly.

Gordon Wallace, rare talent, limited chances.

7

Predictable - like Joe Louis

Liverpool's European career, in the Champions' Cup, began as early as 17 August 1964, with a preliminary round tie in Reykjavik, Iceland. Both St John, ill, and Arrowsmith, injured, were absent, but Gordon Wallace, from the reserves, and Phil Chisnall, a recent signing from Manchester United, deputised. Liverpool took a 5–0 margin back to Anfield for the second leg where a 32,000 crowd cheered the Icelanders heartily – and the Kop gave big Ronnie Yeats some stick – as the visitors went down 6–1.

The first round proper brought a draw against Anderlecht, a team of seven Belgian internationals and Shankly chose this tie in November to launch Tommy Smith. Liverpool had made known their interest in this local schoolboy and one afternoon the boy and his mother appeared at Anfield. Said Mrs Smith: 'This is Tommy. He has lost his father. Look after him.' Even at sixteen, when he made his Central League début, Smith's strength, confidence and long, accurate kicking made him outstanding. Shankly was worried about Anderlecht's attacking abilities, so Smith, wearing number 10, was given a defensive midfield job and Milne a two-fold task: to pick up Anderlecht's star van Himst once he crossed halfway and to attack when Liverpool had the ball. Anderlecht, puzzled, then placed a defender to mark Smith, who was alongside Yeats. In the event Milne had a magnificent match and the Belgians were rocked, 3–0. The second leg brought in a 60,000 gate, but Liverpool had Anderlecht's measure now and a goal from Hunt brought a 4–0 margin. The team of the time were Internazionale of Milan, coached by the magnetic

The man who picked his moment – Tommy Smith, after the European Cup Final, 1977.

Helenio Herrera, who had travelled to Brussels to watch the second leg. Word reached Shankly that Herrera, privately, had hinted he hoped Inter would miss Liverpool.

By now Liverpool were learning to live with the new football. Five attackers had gone for ever, four were a luxury. Teams were settling into 4–3–3 although it would be 1966 and the World Cup before such a formation was accepted. With Smith's arrival Liverpool had arrived at a balanced combination that was capable of adapting to almost any situation: Lawrence, Lawler, Byrne, Milne, Yeats, Stevenson, Callaghan, Hunt, St John, Smith, Thompson. Said Shankly: 'At full strength and in reasonable conditions they were invincible. The best side in Britain since the war.' As ever, Shankly was being contentious, but he had a very strong argument: that the Liverpool team could play superb football and was also learning to win by defence, modern style. Over a programme of ten or more matches they would probably emerge superior to Manchester United (1948 and 1955) or Spurs (1960) in results. Yet they, too, would probably fall to Liverpool (1976) over that same programme and all we would be proving is that the team that wins the most matches is not necessarily the one that wins hearts and leaves memories.

At Christmas 1964 Liverpool abounded with song and football, the whole city was vibrant with a sense of success, achievement and recognition. Even in the League where Liverpool had made an indifferent start – eleven points from fifteen games – the situation had been stabilised by the £40,000 purchase of Geoff Strong, a highly versatile player, from Arsenal. Shankly still believes that the team could have taken on the strain of a triple bid – European Cup, League and FA Cup – had the players he wanted become available. Nowadays it is acknowledged that ambitions of that dimension require a club to maintain a first-team squad of around twenty players and while Liverpool, that Christmas, had a superb first selection they lacked sufficient quality players in reserve. Strong's arrival in November started a run of fourteen games (nine wins) without defeat that guaranteed no worries about their final League place.

The two Cups were the target. The Kop, deciding that Gerry Marsden's version of 'You'll never walk alone' was their very own anthem, were also in superb form and their songs, in those days, were witty as well as sentimental. Very, very rarely could they be tempted to the gutter levels of other clubs' supporters, notably the Stretford End of Manchester United.

1st FC Cologne were the next European opponents and the match was a typical Anglo-German contest. Liverpool, playing no more than three, occasionally two, players forward, forced a goal-less draw on the Rhine. Cologne returned the compliment at Anfield so both clubs went for a play-off to Rotterdam without having scored. This time the goals flowed. Liverpool won a 2–0 lead, Cologne came back to snatch two slim chances and level the game again. Then came the 'Rotterdam roulette'. No satisfactory method had then been evolved for deciding European ties – the penalty method used today has many critics – and the regulation at that time called for the toss-up of a disc, red for Liverpool, white for Cologne. As might be expected from the history of this tie the first spin was inconclusive, the disc sticking on its edge. At the second spin Liverpool's captain Ron Yeats leapt in the air. The disc showed red and his team were in the European Cup semi-final.

Three days later they had to play in the FA Cup semi-final, an example of how events were crowding in on them. The FA Cup run had been far from easy. A 2–1 win at West Bromwich included a penalty miss by Albion; Stockport, bottom club in the Fourth Division, had drawn 1–1 at Anfield, arousing memories of Swansea, before falling 2–0 at Edgeley (Shankly missed the Stockport match at Anfield and his expression, on being told the score on his way to watch Cologne, is said to have been unforgettable.) Callaghan's headed goal beat Bolton in round five.

Dreaded Leicester, with Banks now England's supreme 'keeper, were the quarter-finalists and Liverpool's now practised away tactics brought another goal-less draw. Banks had the Kop spilling over with mingled fury and admiration in the replay and it needed a sudden, devastating shot from Hunt, as he was apparently turning away, to get Liverpool through.

So to the semi-final where the Chelsea of Tommy Docherty, the new blue wave in London, were expected to be much too good for 'tired, jaded' Liverpool. Shankly, of course, never lacked confidence: 'People said we were mechanical, though methodical would have been a better word. They said we were predictable. Being predictable is not too bad, Joe Louis was predictable. He would knock men down on the floor.' London's predictions went sadly awry in the Villa Park semi-final, Liverpool emerging as comfortable 2–0 winners with a Wembley Final against Leeds ahead.

Shankly's plans took a nasty blow at Easter when Milne, who had been having a splendid season alongside St John creating opportunities for Liverpool in midfield, was injured sufficiently to be ruled out of the Final. Strong, who, ironically, had wanted to leave Arsenal because they insisted on playing him in midfield when he believed himself to be a striker, came straight into Milne's place. Lawler had now fitted into right-back in succession to the valiant Moran, Smith forming a central barrier with Yeats that would have frightened King Kong.

The 1965 Cup Final, played on a grey, damp day was a great occasion for Anfield's faithful. Their singing ('God save our gracious team' greeted the Queen) and their fervour made the occasion. The play itself, unless one was a committed Leeds or Liverpool fan, was too careful and cautious to be entertaining. Liverpool planned their first FA Cup victory down to such detail that Shankly even had an empty coach follow the players' coach from Weybridge to Wembley, just in case there should be a breakdown. He said later, 'Leeds were cagey and we took our time. We were not going to be erratic and we took our time. Whether we entertained people or not didn't make any difference.'

What Liverpool couldn't plan happened when Gerry Byrne broke his left collar bone during a fall in one of the early, shattering tackles as both teams sought to reassure the other of their masculinity. Shankly and Paisley gambled, kept Byrne at left-back and hoped Leeds wouldn't notice. They didn't. Byrne won immortal fame on Merseyside with his display ('Gerry's bones were grinding together,' said Shankly afterwards). St John broke the grim, tactical battle with his second goal in extra time, for 2–1, and Liverpool's supporters, many of whom were openly crying, saw the FA Cup as theirs after eighty-one years of trying.

Half of Merseyside was still decorated in red and white when, three days later, Inter Milan arrived for the first leg of the European Cup semifinal. Liverpool were now without both Milne and Byrne and after the emotional outburst of the previous weekend the feeling was that Liverpool would be out-matched by the sinister, subtle and very adept Italians. Moran returned in place of Byrne and Shankly, in an inspired moment of propaganda, with Inter on the field, sent out Milne and Byrne to carry the FA Cup round the ground before the assembled 54,000 on that Tuesday evening. The response was what the team needed to lift them. Hunt first, then Callaghan made it 2–0 before Mazzola pulled one back. St John restored the two-goal margin before the end. The Kop thought the

Geoff Strong, a player for all seasons. His arrival, in 1964, triggered a run of
fourteen games without defeat.

OPPOSITE The long wait is over – the FA Cup is won, 1965.

occasion worthy of its own tribute and, to the melody of 'Santa Lucia', hastily improvised:

> Oh, Inter, One, Two, Three
> Go back to Italy

The second leg, Shankly recalled, 'wasn't a game, it was a war'. Liverpool stayed on Lake Como and had to ask for the interminable church bell-ringing, up till midnight, to be curbed and got a refusal. At the San Siro stadium the reception was worse. Ron Yeats, still saddened by that night, recalled:

We were supposed to be drug-takers, monsters and maniacs. There were bonfires on the terraces and rockets whizzing into the pitch at our feet. And as for that referee from Spain. He signalled an indirect free kick, the ball went straight into our net and he signalled a goal. Their second came after the ball had been kicked out of Tommy Lawrence's hands. Their winning goal was fair enough ... but what a way to win a match!

So a great season ended in disappointment. The achievements had been spectacular. In sixty matches in all competitions Liverpool won twenty-nine and lost only sixteen, had won the FA Cup and equalled Manchester United's achievements in the European Cup. The club's books showed a profit of more than £50,000 on the season, the team was at its peak and entered 1965–6 in powerful and confident style.

Only two home League games were lost and Liverpool were well into their stride by late October. They beat Forest (4–0), Sheffield Wednesday, Northampton (5–0) and then Blackburn (5–2), took over the First Division leadership until they won their seventh championship by defeating Chelsea 2–1 on the last day of April.

Yet once again their domestic power was insufficient to win a European trophy. This time they had been translated to the Cupwinners' Cup and, playing without the injured Lawler and Milne, were happy to escape from Juventus with only a 1–0 defeat in the preliminary round first leg. Lawler and the valuable Strong saw Liverpool through into the first round proper where Standard Liège were beaten by a handsome 5–2 margin. The famous Honved of Hungary could not live up to their reputation (the now familiar, 0–0, 2–0 formula disposed of them) in the quarter-final and the semi-final draw brought a tie that electrified Britain – Celtic of Glasgow.

Eric Roberts, a popular chairman.

Peter Robinson, General Secretary and a key figure in Liverpool's rise.

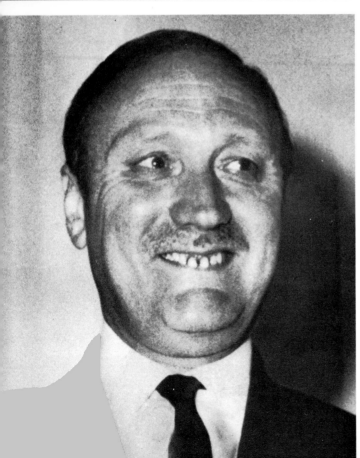

Chairman John W. Smith.

The match was billed, not altogether incorrectly, as the championship of Britain and Liverpool, on their own admission, were lucky to leave Parkhead only one goal down. They were without the durable Hunt, so rarely injured, and shorn of his force and mobility their attack was puny, throwing extra strain on a defence that looked far from confident from the start. Liverpool's players were rightly confident that Celtic would not be able to hold them at Anfield. Smith scored from a free kick and the half-fit Strong headed the winner. Glasgow's revenge came in the Final, against Borussia Dortmund at Hampden Park when a large contingent of Celtic fans came prepared to cheer on the Germans. Hunt had an ankle injury but still managed to score, but on a wild, wet night the Germans were too determined and too well drilled in the counter-attack to be beaten. 'We didn't play well and we gave away two silly goals. The Germans got the breaks and that was it,' admitted Shankly.

The football world was changing fast. That summer England were to win the World Cup with a 4–3–3 formation that effectively put wingers out of British football for ten years. Ronnie Yeats had some telling comments on the trends (1970): 'Since England won the World Cup with a defensive formation the game has gone steadily that way. Liverpool were the first team to put teamwork before individual skills. Leeds followed us, now Arsenal and other clubs are going the same way. I wouldn't be a forward in the 1970s for all the tea in China. I feel sorry for the fans, too.'

Hunt, Byrne and Callaghan were all in England's final twenty-two, although only Hunt won a place in the England Final team. And the FA Cup? That season is not too well remembered, Liverpool were knocked out in the third round, 2–1 by Chelsea – and at Anfield!

In four seasons Liverpool had won the championship twice, won the FA Cup, reached the Cupwinners' Final and the European Cup semi-final; the gate average hovered around 50,000, the profit soared to £148,000. So perhaps it's not surprising that one supporter, thirty-five-year-old Peter O'Sullivan, was so carried away by the birth of a daughter in April 1966 that he had the child registered as Paula St John Lawrence Lawler Byrne Strong Stevenson Callaghan Hunt Milne Smith Thompson Shankly Bennett Paisley O'Sullivan. Such chauvinistic extravagance cannot be explained lucidly or logically in Cheltenham or Surbiton. Arthur Hopcraft, in his superb book *The Football Man*, came closest to the explanation:

We have a plainsong of the terraces. It was created in Liverpool where the city character, with its pervading harshness of waterfront life and bitterly combative Irish exile content, was given a sudden flowering with the simultaneous rise of its pop musicians and of both its leading football teams. More than any other English city, Liverpool experiences its hope and shame through its football.

Vivid memories are frozen in my mind of crowd scenes; the sight of a small, ragged boy appearing gracefully on the skyline of the Kop's acutely slanting roof, stepping gracefully down and sitting down, arms folded, a tiny, symbolic representative of the bravura of his people.

Just as a Gordon or Douglas, a Bruce or Neville, a Stuart or Windsor, Paula O'Sullivan, little lady of Liverpool, had been ennobled.

The mighty Emlyn – always a winner.

Tony Hateley, a song for the Kop.

8

New Blood

The world of football caught up with Shankly and Liverpool in 1966–7. Their lead of almost five years was whittled away by the constant effort, the constant striving, the continual lifting of targets and the ultimate flattery of imitation.

Back in the European Cup it took them three attempts to dispose of Petrolul of Ploesti and then followed the shock of Amsterdam. Ajax, later to dominate Europe, first registered in Britain on a foggy night in December when the mighty Liverpool crashed 5–1. Liverpool, 2–0 down, had Stevenson and Strong raiding forward. The visibility was so poor that Shankly was able to walk on to the pitch, pull back both players, and walk off again without being seen. The manager declared publicly that his Liverpool was still capable of retrieving a four-goal deficit at Anfield. In the event, with a young Johan Cruyff probing either side of Yeats, Liverpool were thought lucky to get a draw. A jubilant Evertonian rang the *Daily Express*: 'Ajax kills all known germs.'

No one, least of all Liverpool's opponents, would admit that a great team was in decline but time and the scars of a hundred battles were telling. Hunt, having played through the World Cup, was clearly in need of a rest. In the FA Cup Liverpool had their rocky moments against Watford and Aston Villa before taking the knock-out from Everton. A week after the cup knock-out Shankly dropped both Milne and Stevenson, the start of an arid spell in which Liverpool failed to score in four successive matches and thus surrendered their championship.

Shankly and Paisley knew that the team had to be rebuilt. One signifi-

Larry Lloyd, who rose from
the reserves to win England
caps.

Alec Lindsay, of the superb
left foot, proving that he
can use the other.

Ray Clemence in full flight.

Alun Evans, the meteor bought
by Shankly for £100,000.

cant figure appeared at Anfield, Emlyn Hughes, a nineteen-year-old left-sided defender from Blackpool whom Shankly had pursued for eighteen months. Liverpool had to pay a club record fee of £65,000 to get Hughes, a record that was to be cracked open time and again in the next few years. The decline in goal-scoring was a major worry. With Hunt fading, St John anchored in midfield and such reserves as Arrowsmith, Graham and Wallace all showing both promise and regular injuries, another major signing was needed. David Wilson, an outside-right from Preston and the Wrexham full-backs, Peter Wall and Stuart Mason, were signed without breaking through to a regular first-team place. Two players who might have given Shankly instant balance and success eluded him: Howard Kendall, almost certainly the best player never to have been capped by England, moved from Preston to Everton. Gordon Banks, hero of the Kop, was sold by Leicester to Stoke.

The spring of 1967 was then a season of discontent. The team, clearly, was in transition and the high fervour of the year before had ebbed among the crowd, too. When Blackpool, already relegated, won 3–1 in the final League game at Anfield, the crowd had fallen to 28,000. Shankly knew that the team would have to be broken up quickly, a task, he once told me, he hated more than any other in management: 'Telling a player who has given his heart for the club that he has to go.' But go they did – Milne to Blackpool, Stevenson to Stoke. Smith and Hughes were to form the new half-backs, stronger in defence but nowhere near as creative as the pair they displaced, a reflection of the times. And perhaps the final measure of Liverpool's achievements was the fact that finishing fifth – and winning a place in the European Fairs Cup – was regarded as a minor disaster.

Shankly made two major signings in the summer of 1967, one that commanded great publicity and another that passed almost un-noticed. He paid Chelsea £96,000 for their tall centre-forward Tony Hateley. 'He looked,' said Bill, 'as if he would be the answer to everything.' Hateley, superb in the air, was soon a favourite with the Kop, but like many other marked strikers of his time he took a tremendous battering from defenders and, because of repeated injuries, had problems in maintaining the standard of fitness that Liverpool required. Sadly, after a year, he moved on to Coventry, the beginning of a round of clubs that produced the Liverpool crack: 'Tony Hateley? He's had so many clubs he doesn't bother to change houses. He lives in a furniture van on the M6.' Shankly also paid Scunthorpe £18,000 for a tall, lean, shy goalkeeper, Ray Clemence.

The lad was, football decided, just a stand-by until Liverpool had decided on the long-term replacement for Tommy Lawrence. Hateley and Clemence, with Hughes who had already arrived, represented the first moves in rebuilding a team that could win trophies, a transition that took three seasons yet a period in which Liverpool were usually threatening in one direction or another.

Season 1967–8, for instance, is remembered around Anfield as one of failure. In fact Liverpool finished third in the First Division, reached the last eight of the FA Cup and continued their European travels. In November, in the second round of the Fairs Cup, Munich 1860 were hammered 8–0 at Anfield, perhaps the last great fling of the swinging side of the 1960s. On New Year's Day 1968, the lean and talented Hungarians from Ferencvaros ended Liverpool's continental interest. West Bromwich, fast replacing Leicester as Liverpool's bogy, won the FA Cup quarter-final after a replay at Maine Road and as the 1968–9 season began Shankly was recruiting again. This time he paid Wolves £100,000 for an eighteen-year-old striker, Alun Evans. 'He had everything necessary to be a great player.' Liverpool, with Evans, hit ten goals in their next two League games, Evans scoring twice and Shankly had seemingly struck gold. It was the impetus Liverpool needed to make an even stronger bid for the League, this time finishing second but, significantly, they were six points behind Leeds and failed to get a man among the ten leading First Division scorers. The European campaign ended on the loss of the toss of a disc to Bilbao, so Liverpool did at least pay their debt to history and Cologne. The old enemy Leicester ended the FA Cup run in the fifth round. Shankly's swoops on Wrexham for two full-backs and on Scunthorpe for a goalkeeper were followed by more excursions into the lower divisions in 1969. Two defenders, Alec Lindsay from Bury and Larry Lloyd from Bristol Rovers, were signed for fees of more than £50,000 and both went straight into Liverpool's reserves.

Time was overtaking Liverpool and Shankly. The rebuilding would have to be accelerated as Liverpool slipped to fifth place in the League, were knocked out of the Fairs Cup by a highly skilful Portuguese team from Setubal (at Anfield) and then suffered the greatest shock within the memory of many followers: an FA Cup knock-out at Watford. Shankly recalled: 'That was the crucial game. Peter Thompson and Tommy Smith didn't play but it was obvious that while some of the players still had an appetite for success others hadn't and might do better elsewhere.' Liverpool had lost that fine full-back Gerry Byrne through injury and were now to lose, through non-selection, Tommy Lawrence and such giants as Yeats, Hunt and St John.

The new decade brought a stirring of the new power at Anfield. A defence was built around Clemence, Lawler, Smith and Hughes; Callaghan and Strong were still in midfield, Thompson was still scything defences on the flanks and young Evans still had the ebullience and talent to upset defences. Another striker was needed and this time Shankly turned to Cardiff to pay £110,000 for the big Welsh international John 'Tosh' Toshack. The press were intrigued by the arrival in Liverpool's reserves of two university graduates, Brian Hall and Steve Heighway, soon to be known to the rest of the players as 'Little Bamber' and 'Big Bamber' after Bamber Gascoigne, quizmaster of a TV show 'University Challenge'.

So 1970–1 became a flexing of the muscles at Anfield. They had only just scraped into the Fairs Cup, but they made Europe remember them with a stirring march to the semi-final. First came revenge over Ferencvaros and it was in a Budapest hotel where Shankly convulsed the whole party. Visibly annoyed at the slow restaurant service to his players he suddenly turned on the waiters: 'What's the trouble? Can't you understand? Are you all foreigners?' Dinamo Bucharest were disposed of in the second round, Evans suffering an injury in Bucharest that was to severely handicap his career, Heighway, advancing so quickly, was able to make his European début in the second leg. Another local forward had appeared, too, in Phil Boersma, to hit the winner against the Rumanians. By the third round (Hibernian of Edinburgh) Toshack had arrived to join the new scorers, but it was Evans who returned to hit a brilliant hat-trick in the quarter-final rout of Bayern Munich, soon to become European champions. The great disappointment was the semi-final. Leeds, who had overtaken Liverpool as the premier English team as the Yeats–St John team faded, were the opponents. To win, Liverpool had to build a substantial lead in the first leg at Anfield, but in fact found themselves 1–0 down and Leeds were far too well organised to concede anything at Elland Road.

The FA Cup campaign was even more promising. Humble Aldershot were despatched 1–0 at Anfield, Swansea followed them, losing 3–0 thus wiping out memories of 1964, and a third home draw, in the fifth round, ended Southampton's interest. For a fourth successive tie Liverpool were

ABOVE The Bard of Anfield, poetry-lover John Toshack, addresses the Coventry defence.

LEFT 'Little Bamber' – Brian Hall.

OPPOSITE ABOVE 'Big Bamber' – Steve Heighway, always an exciting player.

OPPOSITE BELOW Local lad, Phil Boersma.

at home to Spurs in the quarter-final and this time the hurdle proved a little more difficult, for Liverpool had to score the only goal of the tie to win the replay at White Hart Lane. The semi-final draw electrified Merseyside – Everton at Old Trafford and it was a sign of Liverpool's resurgent power that the winning goal, in a 2–1 victory, was scored by yet another recent addition to the first team, 'Little Bamber' Hall. So Liverpool were back at Wembley, this time to face an Arsenal team who had pipped Leeds to the championship by one point and who fancied themselves strongly to follow neighbours Tottenham to the League and Cup double. Yet Liverpool had every reason for confidence. The new defence had conceded only twenty-four First Division goals. The League challenge would certainly have been stronger but for a string of injuries that removed Lindsay, Callaghan, Evans, Thompson and Graham for spells. Conversely those same injuries had accelerated the promotion of Heighway and Hall. The former had already been capped, by the Republic of Ireland, while Yeats's successor Lloyd had become an England player. Just before that Final against Arsenal, in May 1971, Shankly made his greatest signing – after thinking about it for eighteen months.

9

The Boy on the Dustbin

Andy Beattie, an old friend and team-mate of Shankly and part-time scout for Liverpool, had been mentioning an eighteen-year-old at Scunthorpe for almost two years. Does lightning strike twice? Liverpool had, after all, found Clemence, shortly to succeed Banks as the world's number one goalkeeper, in Scunthorpe. Could there be another gem there? One by one, all Liverpool's training and coaching staff watched Kevin Keegan, home and away from the Old Show Ground. Beattie was adamant and eventually Shankly agreed to pay Scunthorpe £35,000. 'It was,' admitted Bill afterwards, 'robbery with violence.'

So the young, small Keegan arrived at Anfield just as the huge new grandstand was being built in the spring of 1971. While the transfer was being completed Keegan, delighting photographers, sat on a dustbin outside the offices – 'Well, they are signing a load of rubbish,' he joked. Shankly, probably still doubtful, took Keegan for his medical examination and that convinced the manager. When he returned he told the office staff: 'He may look nothing dressed but he's built like a tank.'

Liverpool took Keegan to Wembley with them where the team almost selected itself: Clemence, Lawler, Lindsay, Smith, Lloyd, Hughes, Callaghan, Evans, Heighway, Toshack, Hall with Thompson replacing Evans in extra time. Arsenal's luck held. They had squeezed into the Final through a replay won by a last-minute penalty and although Liverpool took them to extra time their defence contained all but Heighway. In retrospect Arsenal's 2–1 margin was decisive and Liverpool had to look back on an astonishing run of near misses: third in the League, a European

The superstar: Kevin Keegan.   An incisive mind – Peter Cormack.

semi-final and an FA Cup Final. Shankly noticed how upset Keegan looked at Liverpool's defeat: 'He probably thinks that if he had been playing we would have won – and we would have done!' Keegan in training left Shankly overjoyed: 'He wanted to be bloody first at everything. Boy, was he keen to be fit.'

In the summer of 1971 Shankly despatched sixteen players under Paisley and the coaches for a short tour of Scandinavia. Keegan was played Callaghan-style at number 8, as a defensive winger. After all, he had been signed as a midfield player. Significantly, his appetite was such he still managed to score twice on the tour. Back home, pre-season, Keegan was moved up to attack in the reserves and after scoring twice was promoted to the first-team forwards for the pre-season First Team *v* Reserves at Melwood. The Reserves, Central League champions for three successive seasons, were shattered 7–1, Keegan scored three and when season 1971–2 opened, against Forest, Keegan was a First Division player.

What finally convinced Shankly and his coaches that they had something special in Keegan was the word of Ian Ross, a versatile player who served Liverpool (and Aston Villa) well without establishing himself at Anfield. Ross was often used by Liverpool to mark opposing stars. Ross told Shankly, of Keegan: 'He's a hell of a hard boy to tab. He's twisting and turning all the time, he's so quick and you never know what he'll do next.' Add Keegan's astonishing stamina, zest, tactical sense and finishing ability and Liverpool had their first – since Liddell – genuine, to use the newly fashionable word, superstar. His impact on the First Division was sensational. He scored in that first game and the media, desperate to find an alternative to the souring story of George Best, seized on Kevin ecstatically. Keegan won his first England under-twenty-three cap in February and by the end of that season was collecting awards from every direction. Shankly described him well: 'He was thrown into the fire and he ignited the new team. He brought it to life with awareness and skill. He was the inspiration.'

Yet even Keegan couldn't lift Liverpool to a trophy in 1971–2, splendidly as the team played for most of the season. The championship was missed by one point, the vital matches coming at Derby, home of the ultimate champions, where Liverpool, 1–0 down, were refused a genuine penalty appeal and at Arsenal, the crucial goal being ruled offside. The FA Cup campaign ended in the fourth round with a replay defeat by those eternal rivals Leeds and the European adventure, in the Cupwinners

(Arsenal having elected to compete among the European champions), was halted by the now fast emerging Bayern, Gerd Muller scoring twice in Munich.

Before Liverpool were to create new frontiers for British football, in 1972–3, Shankly made a surprising signing, Peter Cormack, from Nottingham Forest. Cormack was a skilled and subtle Scottish international but there seemed no obvious place for him at Anfield. Shankly explained why he had spent £110,000: 'If a player of good calibre becomes available you have to be in the market, because they don't come very often.' Cormack, in essence, was a top quality reinforcement. Liverpool had realised that challenging on four fronts – League, FA Cup, Europe and, admittedly unsuccessfully, the League Cup, needed a substantial pool of international players. The test of Shankly's new team and of his European theories was imminent.

Keegan scores against Moenchengladbach, UEFA Cup Final, 1973.

Phil Thompson, a sense of occasion.

10

The Last Minute Lions

We had devised a system of play which minimized the risk of injuries. The team played in sections of the field, like a relay. We didn't want players running the length of the field stretching themselves unnecessarily, so our back men played in one area and so on, to the front men. So whilst there was room for individuals within our system, the work was shared out.

That was Shankly on his team at the start of 1972–3, a season in which Liverpool was to achieve what no other British club had done before. The basic principles remained the same: 'We played to our strengths. We pressurised everyone and made them run. We didn't concede many goals and we didn't score as many as we should have done because we had the opposition backing up.' Shankly taught them patience, too: 'It might take you eighty minutes to win but don't get frustrated because ninety minutes is a long time.' Thus was born the legend of Liverpool the last-minute winners. Opposing teams, and opposing crowds, became sick with apprehension in the final ten minutes: on nine occasions that season Liverpool scored in the final five minutes.

The new team played so well that season that Liverpool even had a run in the League Cup, and defeated Carlisle, West Bromwich and, to the Kop's glee, Leeds before Spurs administered the usual knockout. The FA Cup brought disappointment too, a fourth-round defeat by Malcolm Allison's Manchester City, at Maine Road in a replay, being perhaps the only setback in a golden season. Brian Clough's departure undoubtedly shook the current League champions Derby, but even Clough and his fine team of 1971 would have needed seven-league boots to have stayed with Liverpool that season. They finished three points ahead of Arsenal and no less than seven ahead of third-placed Leeds and such was their strength they were able to crunch up their Saturday League opposition and still turn their power on European rivals in midweek.

In late 1972, in the re-named UEFA Cup, they disposed of Eintracht Frankfurt, AEK Athens and Dynamo Berlin. They began again in March, knocking out Dynamo Dresden and then met Spurs in the semi-final. This was a hard contest. Lindsay gave Liverpool a one-goal lead at Anfield before Spurs appeared to have won the second leg and the tie with two goals from Martin Peters at White Hart Lane. Along came Heighway to score on one of his favourite grounds and Liverpool were into the Final on the away goals' rule.

Borussia Moenchengladbach then, in Shankly's estimation Europe's best club side, were Liverpool's opponents in the Final. Only twenty-seven minutes of the first leg had been played at Anfield when the Austrian referee decided that the continuous heavy rain made further play impossible.

On 10 May the match began again but with a significant difference. Shankly decided to replace the industrious Hall with the tall Toshack, a tactical move that won Liverpool their first European trophy. Said Shankly: 'The German defenders weren't very big and never left their penalty box. Once John started flicking the ball on with his head to Kevin the match was won.' Keegan had scored twice by the thirty-third minute, Lloyd made it 3–0 and to complete a triumphal night at Anfield Clemence saved a penalty. The second leg was much tighter than Liverpool anticipated. Inspired by the great Netzer, Borussia pulled two goals back. Yet the effort drained them and two very tired teams played out a score-less second half, Liverpool's travelling support being joined by several thousand British servicemen, all ready to sing 'You'll never walk alone' as the first European trophy wore Liverpool's colours. Shankly's men returned home to enjoy the adulation and status not accorded any club since Manchester United had won the European Cup in 1968.

They were the top team and, of course, the top target, a distinction that was to be remembered in 1973–4 as Liverpool strove to enlarge the empire. This was to have been the season when Liverpool won the crown of crowns, the European Cup, but that went sour as early as October. A team of tough Luxemburg part-timers, Jeunesse d'Esch, made Liverpool fight for a first-round victory. Hall scored in the customary away leg draw but the Anfield margin was only 2–0 and one of those goals was scored by a Jeunesse defender. The surprise was to come. Red Star Belgrade had a distinguished record in Europe and that season they had an outstanding coach, Miljan Miljanic – later to revitalise Real Madrid. Lawler scored in a 2–1 defeat in Belgrade. 'We come to attack,' proclaimed Miljanic as Red Star flew in and attack they did, shaking Anfield by repeating the score.

Changes were on the way, even in Shankly's new team. When the Celtic and Scotland forward Macari became available Shankly was in first with a £200,000 offer and Macari visited Anfield. He must then have established a precedent by spurning Shankly and signing for Manchester United. In Liverpool's defence the long-legged England youth international Phil Thompson replaced the injured Lloyd, forming a new centre-back partnership with Hughes, while Lawler was about to surrender his right-back place to Smith.

Leeds were thundering away in the League, Dave Mackay had revived Derby's confidence and Liverpool found the iron consistency of the previous season hard to maintain. The League Cup once more promised a run, until Wolves ended Liverpool's chances at Molineux in the quarter-finals and it wasn't until January, and the FA Cup, that Shankly's men moved with their old assurance again.

The Master: RIGHT in expressive
mood with Ronnie Moran;
BELOW shortly before retirement,
leading out the 1974 FA Cup
Finalists.

11

Does a Tiger retire?

Liverpool's near invincibility in front of the Kop was severely tested right at the start of the 1974 FA Cup run. Doncaster Rovers, Keegan's home town team, were winning 2–1 in the third round with twenty-five minutes left to play. Keegan, fittingly, got the equaliser, to be met afterwards by Shankly in prophetic mood: 'That's perhaps the most important goal you'll ever score. Not only will it give the people of Doncaster the chance to see you play it might also win us the Cup.' Liverpool won the replay, then had to repeat the experience, for Carlisle forced a 0–0 draw at Anfield and had to be beaten at Brunton Park. Then came the big fish. Ipswich, always a tactical problem, were swept aside at Anfield and Bristol City beaten at Ashton Gate. Those old, old rivals Leicester were the semi-final opponents and contested as ably as ever, forcing the Old Trafford match into a replay at Villa, where Liverpool finally asserted their superiority. The other Wembley Finalists were Newcastle United.

Shankly believes the 1974 Cup Final was won at Newcastle, not at Wembley. In the First Division match there Liverpool had used the big St James's Park pitch in continental fashion, stringing passes together, five or six at a time. Liverpool didn't score on that occasion – Alan Waddle, a gangling youngster from Halifax was the trialist striker that day – but Shankly claimed seven scoring chances and knew he could beat Newcastle on Wembley's wide open spaces.

The Final was a disaster for Newcastle. Liverpool were so superior they won almost effortlessly. Shankly had won the propaganda battle by such a margin that if Liverpool had failed to turn up they would still have taken the Cup home. Shankly recalls Liverpool's twelve consecutive passes – on the thirteenth Keegan had the ball in the net. The final margin was 3–0 and Newcastle were so poor that Liverpool have never received the credit for playing so well. Except, of course, on Merseyside. A crowd of 250,000 greeted them and Shankly told them: 'You won the Cup.' At that moment in his life, only weeks before his retirement, his rapport with the football folk of Merseyside had never been greater. He could react to the most extravagant gestures with dignity as when two Liverpool fans, at Wembley, insisted on kissing his shoes – 'It was respect for Liverpool.' The previous year, in front of the Kop, he had chided a policeman for screwing up a supporter's scarf: 'Don't do that. It's somebody's life.'

It was Shankly's life, too. He had the Cup, his team, despite what was supposed to be a lesser performance, was second in the League and after forty years in the game he wanted a rest. Before the news broke he insisted on one more big signing, Ray Kennedy, the twenty-two-year-old Arsenal striker, for £200,000. Kennedy, tall, strong and mobile, seemed at first to be a superfluous reinforcement, just a strengthening of the squad, but Shankly and Paisley had seen more to him than frontal attacking.

Liverpool did their best to dissuade Shankly from retirement, offering him another contract on completely his own terms, but he was adamant. John Smith, who had followed Eric Roberts as chairman, was well aware that this was a critical moment for the club. How do you replace a legend? Shankly suggested that his long-standing lieutenant Bob Paisley replace him as manager and that the other coaches, Joe Fagan, Ronnie Moran and Reuben Bennett, followed by Roy Evans and youth coach Tom Saunders, should all move up. The Board agreed. Shankly wanted continuity: 'I knew if someone was brought in from outside it would disrupt the place. It's throwing in a cat among the hens – the hens will fly over the bloody top.' There was, too, 'The Bible', the book kept at Melwood where, at Shankly's insistence, everything of note was recorded, bad times, good times, goals scored, goals missed, injuries and heartaches. So, if a situation arose that needed a quick decision Shankly or Paisley or one of the coaches could always say: 'It's similar to what happened three years ago.' And there it would be, in the book, with notes of the decision taken and the outcome, mostly successful.

Melwood, the great new ground at Anfield, the team, the trophies, all were Shankly's legacy and it was understandable that there should be repercussions following the departure of such a great manager. Where

Liverpool were fortunate was in the presence, in any transitional period, of a highly competent and diplomatic secretary in Peter Robinson. Keegan recalled:

Where Shanks was out of order was in not showing more tact during the early part of Bob's tenure as manager. Bob had just taken on the hardest job in football. To be replacing Bill Shankly, everybody said he was on a hiding to nothing, that he was no more than a sparring partner for a couple of rounds until the club found someone else.

When we went to Melwood Shanks would be there, quite rightly using the facilities. The players would come into training and say 'Good morning, Boss' to Shanks and then 'Good morning, Bob' to Paisley. It was embarrassing.

Keegan also believed that the club had handled the parting badly. Shankly was bitter:

I packed up going to Melwood and I also stopped going into the directors' box at Anfield. I still go to matches, of course. I sit in the stand. I would have loved to have been invited to away matches but I waited and waited until I finally became tired of waiting. Finally after twenty months and after Liverpool had won the League championship again I was invited to travel to Bruges for the second leg of the UEFA Cup Final. I accepted, because I didn't want anyone to think I was petty but it came too late for my peace of mind. I couldn't help wondering why it had taken them so long. And I was not impressed with the arrangements they made for me in Bruges where I was put into a different hotel from the one used by the official party. I found that quite insulting.

In fact the Liverpool club were in an impossible position. The truly great man who relinquishes power and influence gracefully is a rarity in history. Shankly, in football, was a very great man. Does a tiger retire? Liverpool were all too aware of what can happen to a club, no matter how rich and mighty, in the awkward moment when a great man steps down. Manchester United elevated Sir Matt Busby to the Board of Directors on his retirement from management, but the team was still Busby's and two managers, Wilf McGuinness and Frank O'Farrell, were to pay for that with their jobs, while United were relegated. Liverpool may have upset Shankly, and Shankly's players, by making the break in the way they did, but their total commitment to Paisley effected one of the most orderly and successful transfers of managerial power in football history.

The club's enormous debt to Shankly remains. In time they must find

Who scored? Actually it's Kevin Keegan, during the 1974 Cup Final.

some means of honouring him, as they honoured John McKenna. Perhaps the Shankly Gates or the Shankly Stand. To give the man his true mark in the club's history it is not too much to suggest that the Anfield Road stadium be re-named Shankly Park.

12

'I just helped things along'

With the terrible Shankly gone, other English managers looked forward to the 1974–5 season with some optimism. No club, it was said, could make such a change, without a stumble. There would be a rest, perhaps two or three seasons, from the relentless pressure of the Red Army. Liverpool did stumble, to second place in the League. In the FA Cup they knocked out an ambitious Stoke at Anfield but then fell, by one goal, to Ipswich's strength at Suffolk. Inconsistency was Paisley's major worry: a promising League Cup run ended, after West Ham, Sunderland and Hull had been knocked out, by another one-goal defeat at Wolves. In the Cupwinners' Cup Liverpool overwhelmed the Norwegian club Stromsgodset 11–0 at Anfield, the opposing goalkeeper, Thun, delighting one headline writer who seized on THUN-DERSTRUCK. Then came a 'rubber' match with Ferencvaros of Hungary. The two clubs had each won a previous European encounter and Ferencvaros, with a 1–1 draw at Anfield, were able to win through on the 'away goals' rule after a 0–0 draw in Budapest.

Ninety-one other clubs in English football would have been delighted with such a start but Paisley knew, after what had gone before, that the season had been a disappointment on Merseyside. He started to build his own team. Two lanky but very quick young defenders, Phil Neal from Northampton and Joey Jones from Wrexham were signed. Lawler gave way to Phil Thompson in the central defence. Boersma and Cormack, depending on the tactical situation, vied for midfield attacker and, as the big Toshack showed increasing signs of wear and tear, Kennedy became

ABOVE LEFT Ray Kennedy, a profitable investment and tactical revelation.

ABOVE RIGHT Bob Paisley in celebratory mood.

BELOW Paisley's first signings: Joey Jones, pride of Wales; (*right*) Phil Neal, soon an England full-back.

a vital member of the team. Arsenal had used him as a straightforward front runner. Liverpool played him deeper and he would often spend the early part of the match in a defensive, marking role. Once released his forays, usually from the left, employing his height, weight and startling shooting, often swung the match for Liverpool. It was a ploy the opposition found hard to counter, for they could not afford to keep one man detailed to wait for Kennedy to appear. To add variety to the midfield, Paisley paid his first major fee (£170,000) to Newcastle for Terry McDermott, a Scouse who once stood on the Kop and who had reached Newcastle via Bury.

Paisley also had two aces up his sleeve as the 1975–6 season opened – Jimmy Case, a ferocious worker with a cannonball shot, and David Fairclough, a lean, red-haired kid whose startling acceleration and astonishing shooting led to some of Anfield's most spectacular goals. The shakedown season had given Paisley assurance and confidence, too. The players had always respected his ability and knowledge, but because he was also the man who had to fire Shankly's bullets, he was also sometimes resented. His unerring eye for potential injuries – Keegan heard Paisley predict cartilage operations for players by watching them on TV – was only a part of the Paisley football compendium revealed to the team once he took charge. Deliberately or accidentally, Paisley paced 1975–6 superbly. 'Once we got to know the real Bob our relationship with him was excellent and his confidence grew,' said Keegan, speaking for the dressing room.

Knowing Liverpool faced a formidable programme (the eventual total of competitive games was fifty-nine), Paisley planned the campaign meticulously. In the style of champions Liverpool exerted controlled pressure, sufficient for the task in hand, saving their maximum bursts for the crucial occasions.

Queen's Park Rangers and the newly promoted, attacking Manchester United won the headlines and not until Liverpool's twenty-second match, a 2–0 win against Rangers, did Liverpool take the First Division leadership. Both Rangers and United came back brilliantly and by Easter the London club were the championship favourites. Liverpool had the toughest holiday programme but stormed through it magnificently, smashing Stoke 5–3 at Anfield and defeating the powerful Manchester City 3–0 at Maine Road, Fairclough having an electrifying match. United dropped out the following Wednesday, losing at home to Stoke. Rangers won their final match against Leeds, giving them a one-point advantage over Liverpool, who still had to play their final game at Wolves. That match was sandwiched between the two legs of the UEFA Cup Final against Bruges – as Bob Paisley said: 'We now have to play three Cup Finals.'

FA Cup hopes had crumbled in the fourth round at Derby but in Europe Liverpool were their own confident selves. At Hibernian Liverpool went down 1–0 – despite Ray Clemence's penalty save – but a headed hat-trick by Toshack won the tie at Anfield. Real Sociedad were hit for nine goals in the next round, full-back Brian Kettle and Fairclough making their European débuts; Slask Wroclaw (15 degrees below in Poland!) fell 5–1, a hat-trick coming from Case in the second leg. Old foes Dynamo Dresden popped up in the quarter-finals. Clemence saved another penalty in Dresden, Case and Keegan scoring in the second leg. Barcelona, now with the Dutch maestros Cruyff and Neeskens, made for a glittering semi-final. Clemence's vast goal kick was flicked on by Keegan for Toshack to score past a stretched Barcelona defence. The Spanish fans hurled cushions in disgust at Barcelona's inability to score; Joey Jones, whose experience had been confined to homely Wrexham, retaliated by throwing them back until assured by the Liverpool bench that they were not directed at him personally. Barcelona were a much more fiery proposition at Anfield where Liverpool were happy to draw 1–1 and win on aggregate. The Final was against Bruges of Belgium, who staggered Anfield by taking a 2–0 lead early in the first half. At the interval Paisley produced a masterly tactical switch, replacing Toshack by Case, a move that led Liverpool to a 3–2 lead on the first leg and the Kop feeling they had more than their money's-worth.

The true test of Paisley's team followed. Their next fixture was their remaining League match at Molineux where they needed a draw (up to 3–3) to take the championship. To be absolutely certain that Rangers' superior goal average was nullified, Liverpool needed to win. Wolves led 1–0 at half-time, but Liverpool, exerting all their speed, strength and tactical expertise, turned on such power in the final fifteen minutes that they shattered Wolves with three goals and left a stricken Molineux with no doubts as to the best team in England.

Liverpool took a one-goal lead to Bruges for the second leg of the UEFA Final, plus the pride stemming from the knowledge that they had won the League a record nine times. Even an eleventh-minute penalty by

Terry McDermott – the Kopite
returns.

Jimmy Case, a new dimension to
Paisley's team.

Bruges failed to upset them. Four minutes later Keegan's swerving shot equalised and Liverpool were happy and capable of sitting on a 1–1 draw, to take the UEFA Trophy to Anfield a second time. Bob Paisley, having emulated Shankly's feat of 1973, the League and UEFA Cup in one season, was typically self-deprecating: 'Liverpool have been geared to this sort of thing for fifteen years. I have just helped things along.'

13

The March on Rome - and Beyond

The first move in what was to be the most eventful season in Liverpool's history came in the summer of 1976 when Real Madrid asked Liverpool if they were prepared to transfer Kevin Keegan. Spain had been importing continental stars, at enormous fees and salaries, for two years and it was hardly surprising that British players, reflecting on their income tax, should seek the same opportunities. Keegan had expressed interest publicly in playing abroad. After the Real Madrid approach he met Liverpool chairman John Smith and a compromise was agreed: if Keegan would stay with the club for one more season, one more attempt at the European Cup, then he would be released. That eased Bob Paisley's mind and gave added impetus to Liverpool's vaulting ambitions. Not since the Manchester United of 1957 had England a team of such strength that it could be spoken of as favourites for the League, the FA Cup and a European trophy in one season. Not even that Manchester United, the 'Babes', could, in the event, match Liverpool's achievements in 1976–7: League champions for a tenth time, FA Cup Finalists and then, the supreme triumph, the European Cup.

The 'Double' team of 1975–6 had been reinforced by the signing from Ipswich of the England forward David Johnson, an ex-Evertonian. Johnson was very much part of a tactical permutation, depending on circumstances, with McDermott, Toshack and Fairclough.

Europe opened with an awkward tie – the Belfast club Crusaders. The Irishmen made a gallant impression on Anfield, losing only 2–0 and left many new friends. Said one Irishman, drowning a treble Scotch: 'I fancied seeing Blackpool illuminations. But I don't want to leave the bar tonight so I'll go in the morning.' Crusaders hit Clemence's woodwork twice in Belfast in the first half but Keegan's goal ten minutes after the interval was the signal for the now familiar machine-gun punishment – four more goals in the last nine minutes.

Peter Robinson's administrative abilities (he was promoted General Secretary, a new title to signify his outstanding service to the club) were tested again in October when the draw sent Liverpool to the Turkish champions Trabzonspor on the Black Sea coast. Liverpool had just taken over the First Division leadership, beating Everton 3–1 in the second week of October and despite all the tribulations of Trabzon – travelling, the hotel, training, food, the bumpy pitch and an old match ball were a long, long way from the First Division – returned with a 1–0 (a disputed penalty) deficit. With a three-point lead in the League, Liverpool sailed into the Turks at Anfield, scoring three times in the first eighteen minutes and then they had to wait for the quarter-final draw.

There were enough old friends in the last eight of the European Cup – Bayern Munich, Dynamo Dresden, Borussia Moenchengladbach and Bruges. Yet the draw pitted Liverpool against the new power in Europe, France's champions St Etienne, losing European Cup Finalists (to Bayern) the previous season. A Scouse exile wrote to warn Liverpool *Echo* readers that all France would be behind 'Les Verts' and then cheered the Anfield faithful by adding: 'But they all keep asking "Oo eez deez Fairclough?" ' French newspapers billed the match as 'The Greens' *v* 'The Super Reds' … but Liverpool, without Keegan, who had pulled a ligament, and with Toshack suffering an achilles tendon injury, did their best to take the hysteria out of the fixture. After a couple of speculative shots they dropped anchor and returned to Anfield with a 1–0 deficit. The French suspected, rightly, that they had missed their chance. Keegan was fit again for the second leg (16 March) and Fairclough substituted for Toshack. St Etienne had lost their famous Argentine stopper Piazza, 'The Beast', who had been suspended. Just 102 seconds into the second leg and Keegan drifted a ball over from the left and over the St Etienne keeper: 1–1. St Etienne came back brilliantly, Clemence made two electrifying saves, but was beaten six minutes after the interval for the French to regain the lead – and with an away goal. Kennedy levelled the scores again (fifty-eight minutes) and the French were still winning, on that away goal, when Fairclough, re-placing Toshack, appeared and in one brilliant movement he covered

David Fairclough, a bombshell.

David Johnson, back home via Ipswich.

forty yards, swayed past two defenders and then beat the advancing keeper for a goal that had the Kop in raptures. Zurich, the semi-finalists, were an anti-climax after this classic, falling by 20 April to a 6–1 margin. On the other side of Europe Borussia Moenchengladbach ensured an Anglo-German Final in Rome on 25 May.

The strain of Liverpool's three simultaneous campaigns was showing: Toshack was joined among the injured by Phil Thompson and then Callaghan, bringing a recall for the thirty-two-year-old veteran of older glories, Tommy Smith, in the back four. Apart from the sheer emotional and physical pressures of reaching the European Cup Final Liverpool had won their domestic battles, too. Perhaps they were fortunate in the FA Cup draw – Crystal Palace, Carlisle, Oldham and Middlesbrough disputed their path to Wembley – but they were also the champions and intended to remain so. Only in the Cup semi-finals did Liverpool stumble and that was when they were drawn against the oldest foe of all, Everton, who took them to two tight matches at Maine Road before finally succumbing 4–3. There were times when they played like a tired team, especially in the League, but on 11 May, after an uninspired 0–0 draw against a mediocre Coventry, they needed just one point for the championship, a point won four days later against West Ham (another 0–0) at Anfield. There was a strain of sadness in the jubilation for Keegan proclaimed afterwards: 'This is my last match at Anfield.' He was to return, sooner than he expected, with his new club SV Hamburg, but at that time he believed he would be joining either Real Madrid or Bayern Munich.

That was the first part of the Treble. Seven days later Liverpool met Manchester United, defeated Finalists in 1976, for the FA Cup Final at Wembley. At this point Bob Paisley's major worry was team selection; with a European Cup Final three days away the margin for error was enormous. Callaghan was fit again, Fairclough was bursting to play, but in the end the manager went for a blend of youth and experience, McDermott and Johnson, leaving Callaghan as substitute. Was it the wrong decision? That Cup Final suggested that United were fated to win no matter who Liverpool chose. Kennedy headed against the foot of a post in a first half in which Liverpool were the more composed and authoritative team. United took the lead after fifty minutes, Case equalised within three minutes; Macari restored United's lead with a deflection off Greenhoff that stranded Clemence and, finally, two minutes from time, Kennedy hit the angle.

Kenny Dalglish: £440,000 of Scottish steel.

Graeme Souness, strength and skill
from Middlesbrough.

Nothing stirred in the Liverpool dressing-room. There was no banquet. By 7.45 pm the players were on a train back to Liverpool. Said Paisley: 'The lads will have forgotten about Wembley by the time we arrive in Rome. The task there will be even more difficult than Wembley because Moenchengladbach are one of the best teams in the world, let alone Europe.' Then, almost as an afterthought, ex-Desert Rat Bob said something that endeared him to his team and to Merseyside. It was the first, famous Paisleyism: 'The last time I was in Rome was thirty-three years ago. I helped capture it.'

Liverpool were training at Melwood the following Monday morning. A specialist had given Toshack permission to play if needed and that story sent ripples of alarm through Germany for it was Toshack's heading power that had shattered Borussia in the first leg of the UEFA Cup Final four years before. The next day, 24 May, came the flight to Rome. Paisley stuck to his Wembley team, including Callaghan, and could choose two substitutes from Johnson, Fairclough, Lindsay, Toshack and deputy keeper Peter McDonnell. Said Paisley, simply: 'We know this is the chance of a lifetime.' Light training, the morning of the match, saw Toshack break down. Waddle, the 6 ft 3 in reserve striker, replaced him on the bench in the Olympic Stadium that evening when Liverpool were greeted by an estimated and amazing 26,000 followers. Not merely the Stadium but Rome itself belonged to Merseyside. And Rome, unlike London, was lucky. After twenty-two minutes Bonhof hit a fierce twenty-yard shot that beat Clemence, the ball flying off the base of a post and straight into Clemence's arms. Six minutes later Callaghan sent Heighway flying down the right and a measured pass was taken beautifully on the run by McDermott for a resplendent opening goal. Not until six minutes after half-time did Borussia draw level when Simonssen, soon to be European Footballer of the Year, beat Clemence with a magnificently struck high shot. Then Borussia caught fire and for ten minutes Liverpool wavered and it needed a superb save by Clemence, from Stielike, to restore the faith. Three minutes later Heighway's corner kick was headed into the net by Smith at the near post, a sudden move that left Borussia thunderstruck. It shook Smith, too, for it was his first goal of the season on his six hundredth appearance and he commented afterwards: 'I've changed my name to Roy of the Rovers.' Keegan's last move for Liverpool was historic, too. He had been drawing the Borussia defence for much of the match and then, as the match entered the last ten minutes, the time

Hughes holds the European Cup at Tommy Smith's Testimonial Match.

of the lions, Keegan advanced. He suddenly accelerated, darted into the box and a desperate Vogts floored him. Neal, now Lindsay's replacement as the icy taker of penalties, strode up to calmly score the penalty.

The celebrations began there and then and as the joyous news, like good Chianti, flowed through Europe, the cheers, the bells, the whistles, the singing went on through the night. All England was proud of Liverpool, of a team that had done remarkable things, leaving no great rancour among their opponents, no trail of devastation by their supporters. Their virtues, as a team, were very English: dedication, application, unfailing support for the individual, intense loyalty, a willingness to improvise and a rollicking sense of humour. For twelve years Liverpool had been the yardstick by which other English teams were judged. Now all Europe had to measure themselves against the men of Anfield.

And afterwards . . .

14

The Paisley Pattern

The damp, often grey summer of 1977 brought weeks of reflection to Anfield while the now huge army of those who followed Liverpool's fortunes waited expectantly to see what would happen next. Keegan joined Hamburg for £500,000 and was, ironically, a member of the German team decisively defeated by Liverpool in the new European Supercup competition.

On 11 June Paisley (OBE) and Tommy Smith (MBE) joined Shankly (OBE) and Callaghan (MBE) as members of the Order of the British Empire. Bob, indisputably, was Manager of the Year.

On 11 August Liverpool paid a British record fee of £440,000 for the Celtic and Scotland striker Kenny Dalglish, a signing greeted by Keegan, in Hamburg, with: 'He may prove a better player for Liverpool than I did.'

Dalglish went through August scoring on average a goal a game and on 1 September Liverpool's great stature in the national game was recognised by England when Clemence, Callaghan, Neal, Hughes, Kennedy and McDermott were selected against Switzerland along with, of course, Keegan. 'Why not Fairclough?' demanded an irate Liverpool supporter.

By the end of September the euphoria was fading. Liverpool were still collecting points handsomely but almost always through Dalglish's goals and after a lethargic 1–0 home victory over a poor Derby team Paisley warned publicly: 'The party's over.'

What was needed was the European Cup and, on cue, Liverpool donned the harness of champions to shatter their first opponents, Dynamo

Dresden, 5–1 at Anfield. Dynamo were a shade sharper in East Germany where Clemence's immaculate goalkeeping and Fairclough's later intervention brought a satisfactory 1–2 result.

Three days later Aston Villa won at Anfield, a week after Manchester City had beaten Liverpool 3–1 and when Queen's Park Rangers also won 2–0 Liverpool had, amazingly, suffered four consecutive defeats.

'CRISIS' screamed the sports pages, tongue in cheek, while Paisley paid Chesterfield £75,000 for a twenty-year-old goalkeeper Steve Ogorozovic. Phil Thompson's return to fitness was another relief yet it needed another whiff of Europe to restore Liverpool's spirits.

Hamburg, held 1–1 on the Alster, were smashed 6–0 at home, Keegan looking decidedly embarrassed. After Bristol City had cheekily taken a point from Anfield the army began to roll again. Leicester were beaten 4–0 at Filbert Street and although the League results remained wobbly by December the season, and a new team, were taking shape. An attempt was made to sign Middlesbrough's Scottish international midfielder Graeme Souness before the European Cup qualifying date as both McDermott and Case were struggling with injuries. Souness signed for £352,000 on 11 January; Benfica of Lisbon were drawn in the European Cup and the Merseyside public suddenly realised history was also being made, virtually unnoticed.

The League Cup, a competition in which Liverpool had made no previous impression, came suddenly in sight after an uninspired but nevertheless successful campaign that had brought the elimination of three First Division clubs, Derby County, Coventry and the domestic Cup team of the season, Arsenal.

For the seventh time in seven years Liverpool were at Wembley, this time in their first League Cup Final, to meet Brian Clough's shiny new Nottingham Forest, a team that had attracted more attention and praise than any since Manchester United in Busby's hey-day.

League form was still mercurial, Derby winning 4–2, a surprisingly heavy defeat, at the Baseball Ground while Forest continued to career away at the top.

Three days before the Final on 15 March Liverpool disposed of Benfica 4–1 at Anfield in the European quarter–final (they already led 2–1 from Lisbon) and the Paisley team pattern finally emerged: in front of Clemence the back four read Neal, Smith or Hansen, Thompson, Hughes or Jones. In midfield we saw Case, Callaghan or Souness (who

ABOVE The
European Cup Final
at Wembley, May
1978. McDermott
forces his way
through.

Kenny Dalglish
with the cup his
audacious goal
clinched.

had played in the League Cup for Middlesbrough that season), McDermott and Kennedy. And the specialist strikers, two from three, were Dalglish, Heighway or Fairclough.

The strength of Paisley's team lay in the midfield where he had every manager's dream, four players of international class all of whom could tackle, harry, create and score. Add a world-class keeper and a world-class striker, Dalglish, and Liverpool's second successive European Champions' Final was predictable.

First there was Forest. Dalglish, that cool and deadly finisher, missed an early opportunity at Wembley and Forest, with three expensive recruits barred, like Souness, and another defender injured, were happy to contain and wait for a Liverpool error. It came in the replay the following Wednesday at Old Trafford. Thompson brought down a Forest forward on the edge of the box and the penalty goal was sufficient to give Forest the prize. Liverpool were angry as the film of the incident suggested that the foul had been committed outside the area but most impartial observers felt that justice, overall, had been done.

Liverpool, over 180 minutes, had failed to beat a Forest team much under strength and the decisive moment, Thompson's tackle on O'Hare, was by everyone's admission a foul no matter where it took place.

By the end of March Liverpool were taking on their old foes Borussia Moenchengladbach in the European Cup semi-final with Paisley now very conscious of the brinkmanship the team were practising.

A fifth place in the League table was not a guarantee of a place in European football in 1978–9. The channels provided by the FA Cup and League Cup had been blocked and in the European Cup the semi-finals and above are levels at which the gods impose their fickle loves and hates on human destiny. Then Liverpool had a stroke of luck. Simonsen, Borussia's brilliant Danish striker, European Footballer of 1977–8, was injured in a Bundesliga fixture and Liverpool escaped from Dusseldorf just 2–1 down.

Back home they won an enthralling derby at Goodison by 1–0 – Everton had also failed to win the fourteen previous League encounters – and on 12 April, at Anfield, Liverpool made history, becoming the first British club to reach consecutive European Cup Finals by beating Borussia 3–0 in the second leg.

Paisley had to concede the League championship to Forest, a gesture that seemed, almost immediately, to lift a burden from his team. With one target left the players settled into happier form and with a startling run in the final fortnight victories against Manchester City and West Ham ensured second place in the League, a position Evertonians had been confident of occupying since Easter.

The European Cup Final at Wembley on 10 May saw Liverpool as almost the hottest favourites in the tournament's history. Bob Paisley was not amused. He told the *Sunday Telegraph:* 'People were saying that the last eight in this year's European Cup was the strongest for a long time. But, suddenly, it's a non-vintage year again. It's always the same with us; when we beat people easily it must be that they weren't any good anyway or didn't really try. It hurts, not only because we are a good side but because we have always set out to be the best possible ambassadors for our country and for its national game.'

The day before the Final the *Daily Express* recorded Liverpool's European career: 14 successive seasons, 73,000 miles and the match against Bruges was their 99th European tie. Ian Callaghan had played in 89, six short of the record held by the great Gento of Real Madrid. The full playing record read: played 98, won 56, drawn 19, lost 23; goals for 197, goals against 77.

Bruges were short of two injured attackers; Liverpool had to replace the iron Smith, also injured, with Hansen while Heighway, convalescing, was replaced by Fairclough.

The match, said the commentators, was a disappointment. The previous Saturday Ipswich had beaten Arsenal in a classical FA Cup Final and the comparison was, at times, embarrassing. But, as Tommy Smith pointed out: 'It's difficult to play against a team who don't want to play.'

Bruges's containing tactics on a dull, warm evening, survived, against relentless Liverpool pressure, until the sixty-fourth minute. Paisley had just replaced Case with Heighway when McDermott, Souness and Dalglish combined in a move that put Dalglish wide and clear of the defence.

Bruges's brave and quick Danish keeper Jensen came hurtling off his line for Dalglish, finishing as calmly and audaciously as Jimmy Greaves, to chip the ball across him and into the net.

Wembley was delirious while Merseyside, forgetting the factory closures and, the protest marches, exploded into another night of joy.

Emlyn Hughes cast his mind back to Rome: 'Somebody asked me then how we could top winning the European Cup. I said we could start by winning it again.'

'And again.'

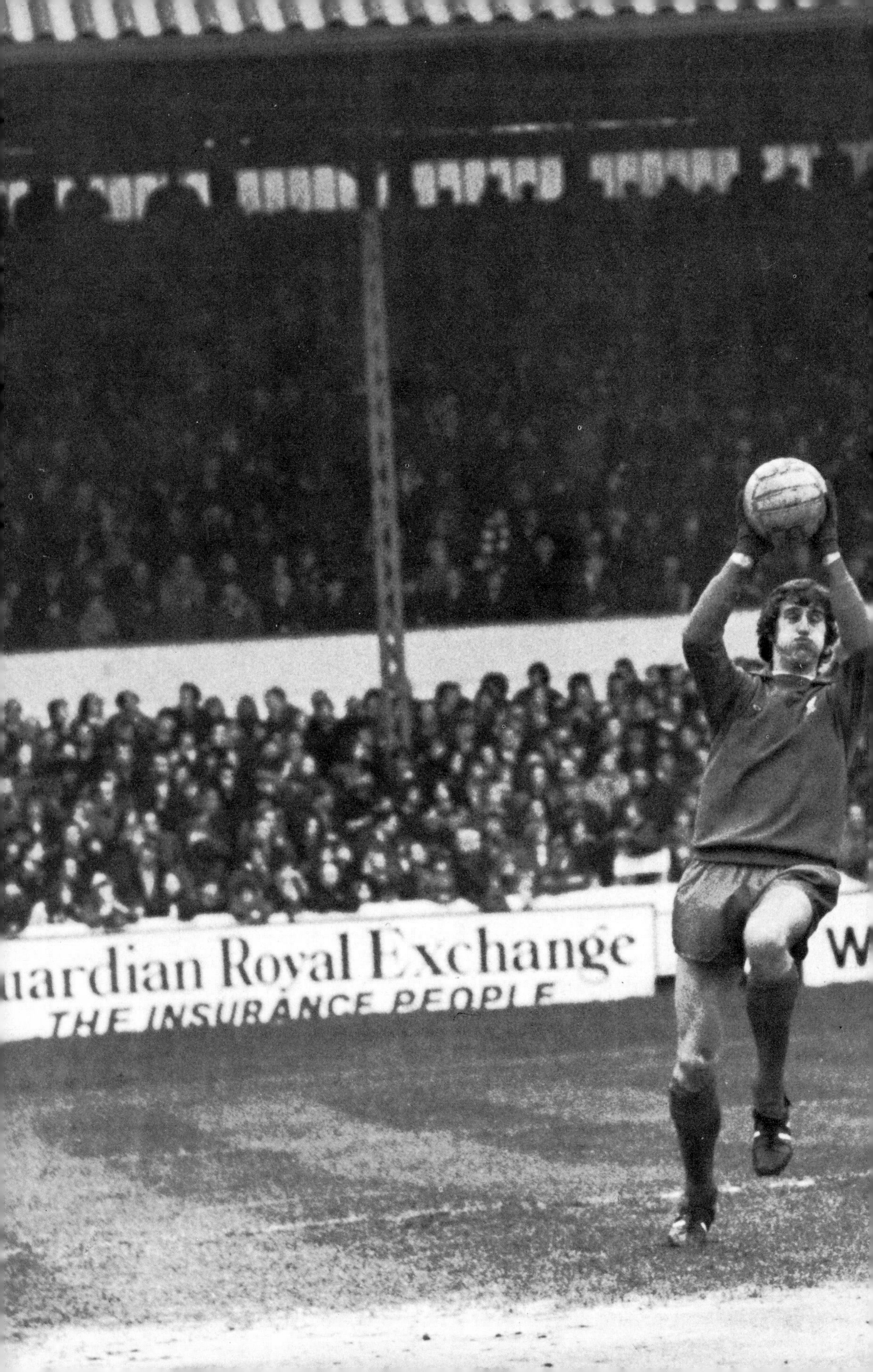
uardian Royal Exchange
THE INSURANCE PEOPLE